Secrets of Your Soul

SECRETS OF YOUR SOUL

A Story of Past Lives Unveils Personal Wisdom Beyond Your Wildest Dreams

Alison Wem

YOUR SOUL FAMILY

connecting with your soul
calmness – harmony - wisdom

First published in 2023 by Alison Wem

Printed and distributed by Alison Wem Publishing
London, UK

Visit Alison Wem's website at www.yoursoulfamily.com.

A catalogue record for this book is available from the British Library.

ISBN: 978-1-9997014-5-1
ISBN: 978-1-9997014-4-4 (ebook)

Copy-editor: Steven Hiatt
Cover design by Jessica Bell
Illustrations by Emma Schultz

Names have been changed to protect the identity and privacy of those involved.

To White Cloud and Lucinda, my dear guides, who have been with me since the beginning of my journey to explore who I am.

Contents

Foreword

Life is an evolutionary journey leading to enlightenment, and incarnation is its means. As human beings, we have experienced countless lives, and each has helped mould us into who we are today. Over the vastness of time, the soul works towards perfecting its relationship with its personality – the lower mind, emotions and body, gradually transforming it into its willing servant. In this way, the soul becomes better able to express its love and wisdom through the personality. This is the reason for reincarnation, for it takes many lifetimes for this perfecting process to be fully achieved.

Rebirth can therefore be viewed as the incarnational pulsation of the soul as it seeks to evolve through the personality, eventually culminating in the experience of enlightenment itself. And when such a lofty state of development is finally attained, the need to return to incarnated life is no longer required, for the personality has been fully transformed, and the soul's expression through it is then unencumbered.

In this beautifully written book, the author presents us with a unique type of case study regarding reincarnation, designed around a dialogue between herself and Andrea's soul. Lessons learned over the course of many lifetimes are intimately and authentically shared, each providing profound insight into the experiences that had occurred in previous incarnations, and how they have shaped her life today.

Secrets of Your Soul is a book that I highly recommend. It is a must read for anyone who desires to see and understand themselves through a multi-incarnational lens, and it provides a variety of methods and practices to help each of us live more soulfully within our current incarnation.

– **William Meader**

International teacher of The Esoteric Wisdom

Oregon, USA, June 2023

Introduction

Have you ever done something and thought you could do it better next time? Or met someone and have been so comfortable with them that you have felt you have known them for ages? The answer is that you probably have. Your level of familiarity with a task or person or place may well come from a past life.

You may have been taught or like to think that at the moment of birth we are all equal. Sadly, I believe this is not the case. You bring into this life the experiences and skills along with the wisdom you have learnt from living previous lives. It's what makes you unique because only you have had your past life experiences and gained the hard-earned wisdom that has come from them. You may or may not be conscious of them, but your subconscious, higher self or, as I prefer to call it, your soul, is very much aware of your previous learnings.

You bring into this life the experiences and skills along with the wisdom you have learnt from previous lives.

When my friend Andrea and I came together in this lifetime, we knew we had something to accomplish together. I was perhaps the slower and the more reluctant party to accept what we needed to do, but Andrea was very persuasive in her argument of our need to walk together. Andrea appeared in my book *Finding Your Soul Family*, providing feedback on the exercises to construct a Soul Map.[1] It was at a time in her life when she

1 **Soul Map:** A visual representation of you and your life. It captures who is in your soul family, the relationships between members and the life lessons you are learning. A Soul Map can guide your personal and spiritual development.

was remembering many past lives. She was exploring why this was so and what she was learning from them. Andrea used Soul Maps to analyse and understand the relationships and life lessons being learnt between members of her soul family.[2] However, Andrea was not ready, at the time of publishing *Finding Your Soul Family*, to share publicly the depth of the learning she had achieved from working her Soul Map. Now she would like to rectify this and share with you the story of her evolution through many past lives, what she learnt by living them and how she came to know she is an eternal being living lives to learn to be her best self. This book, *Secrets of Your Soul*, thus aims to help you develop your enjoyment of life and assist your learning. Indeed, I believe you can continue to learn in this lifetime until the day you take your last breath.

In bringing this book to you, Andrea's and my roles are very different. In our partnership I am the narrator and communicator, whereas Andrea provides the key content and wisdom. Together we complement one another. We have learnt a lot together and experienced the exhilaration of living a life with all its ups and downs – made more endurable by humour and love.

Andrea: When Alison and I agreed to write this book, I put much thought into how to present my past lives to you, so they are coherent and easy to understand. I have found that a past life memory came to me usually when there was a challenge in my current life and there was a skill or experience from a past life that could help me now. Should the story of my past lives be in the order I came to know them in this life, or in the chronological order of the lives?

A past life memory came to me usually when there was a skill from a past life that could help me now.

I like to think of the extended reality of life containing many human lives in this way. When you have a baby, you accept and expect the baby to grow into a toddler, child, adolescent and then an adult. I believe there

2 **Soul family:** The soul group you belong to and typically reincarnate with numerous times. In your current life they can be some of your immediate family but often include wider family, friends and colleagues.

is a second, invisible and not fully accepted, part of you. I call it my soul – others who might be more scientifically minded might call it their subconscious. I prefer *soul* as it is such an intimate part of me and my best friend through the trials of all my lives. We are two halves that make a whole. My story of my past lives is the story of my soul's growth from a baby where he seldom influenced my life, through to adulthood, at which stage we are one. Like a baby growing up, I stumble along as I try to find my path. I have successes and failures. Sometimes I need to retake a life lesson to truly absorb and learn it. At the time I often felt alone in my challenges. It is only now, as I recognise the wider definition of life, that I realise I was loved and nurtured every step of the way.

In sharing my story, I hope that at least parts of it might resonate with you and your soul's growing up. If in any way it makes your growing into leading a fulfilling life easier and more hopeful and gives purpose to your life experiences, I am grateful. Life is for living and enjoying. Learning and growing should be fun. Learning often brings surprises. When you meet your soul, it may bring forth wisdom beyond your wildest dreams. In this learning there are so many helping hands reaching out to you – you just need to place your hand in theirs and trust the love you feel to help you along the way. The wonder and wisdom of this journey is outstanding, which is why I agreed to share mine with you.

Alison: The opportunity of Andrea remembering her lives seemed too good to miss. Andrea has been very open with us and shared her failures as well as her successes. The observer in her has been objective about her lives without being judgemental. It is a personal description of living the wider reality of life rather than an academic treatise or philosophy of the meaning of life. These philosophies do have a place in explaining to you what is happening to you as you evolve, for those who desire it. However, most people's commitment to evolution is to just turn up the next day and to live the next day of their life. There is nothing wrong with this approach. It is a fundamental of life and a prime driver of all life, including the soul.

The observer in Andrea has been objective about her lives without being judgemental.

I would like to thank Andrea for her brutally honest and sometimes amusing account of the evolution of her soul.

How do you describe the discovery of the divine part of you and the evolution of your soul in a way people can understand and want to engage with?

Andrea: I have been and continue to be on this incredible and wondrous journey of my own evolution for expanded consciousness. If I am asked what this journey is, I answer that it's about me – who I am, what I believe in and how I relate to my fellow human beings, the world and the universe that I reside in.

How long have I been on this journey? A defining moment in my life was when my father passed in 1997, followed by many of my close family in rapid succession. So perhaps you might say that this experience created a crisis in my life which brought about my spiritual beliefs, but if I'm honest to myself, I know that it goes back further than then.

Did my journey start when I was eleven years old? I was an asthmatic with pneumonia, suffering a nightly ritual of waking unable to breathe, fighting for my very breath, my face going blue and experiencing a pain in my back as though someone was cruelly stabbing me with a knife. Somewhere inside, when I was attempting to swim across the fluid in my lungs and unable to keep my head above water, I consciously decided it was all too much effort and started to pass. The love, the lightness and the well-being I felt outside of my body was good. It was only my mother's pitiful screams and deep love for me, her child, that called me back.

All through my childhood I chatted quite happily to someone inside me. They were my counsel, my companion, always there and just part of my life.

But my awareness of Spirit had started earlier. All through my childhood I chatted quite happily to someone inside of me. They were my counsel, my companion, always there and just part of my life. I assumed everybody had the same. I discovered that I could influence the throw of the dice to enable me to win games – what fun! My older brother used to get so mad that his little sister could beat him.

As my awareness grew, I started to remember a life in ancient Greece, which is greatly linked to this life, with the same participants. Strangely enough, they all seem to have the same gender today as they had in that Greek life. Former lives and an understanding of their significance to my spiritual growth slowly unveiled themselves to me. Through many lives, I have experienced just about all religions humans have defined. I have been Jewish, pre-Roman Christian, Catholic, Cathar, Protestant, Muslim, Buddhist and many more. Often, I seemed to have adopted the religion which was counter to the prevailing politics of the time. I seemed to want to push the boundaries, continually trying to find the meaning of life.

I have experienced just about all religions. I have been Jewish, pre-Roman Christian, Catholic, Cathar, Protestant, Muslim, Buddhist and many more.

My wonderful soul travel guide husband, who does not believe in all this mysterious theory, took me to key locations from previous lives during our holiday trips. My guide[3] loved to control my husband's satellite navigation system, though, and direct us to specific places of key importance to both of us.

I became aware of healing energy in my hands. I experimented with giving energy to cut flowers to see if I could get them to last as long as if they were still attached to the main plant with their roots in the ground. I found I could influence the traffic lights and when I requested help, stretch time to arrive in the right place on time. People, books and situations started to arrive in my life to jog my memory on what I was here to achieve.

I became acquainted with my main guides more formally. I learnt their names and experienced the humour and personality of my main guide, Wang. I learnt that the universe likes balance and symmetry, and although in many ways mysterious is consistent and reliable. I learnt to build and memorise my Soul Map, which is my own mandala[4] given to me through

---

3 **Guide:** A person in the Spirit world who guides and protects us. Everyone has a guide; you may just not recognise them. Often, it's the person you chat to in your head who helps you in times of stress or if you are in need of company. I chatted to mine for many years before I knew what or who he was. This amused him as he has a great sense of humour.

4 **Mandala:** An ancient Eastern art form, originating around the 9th century. Traditional mandalas, often created by Buddhist monks, can be deeply elaborate representations of nirvana. In Eastern spiritual traditions, mandalas are considered to be maps of the cosmos. Buddhist mandalas are rich with symbolism that can evoke many different aspects of Buddhist teaching.

meditation[5] and intuition.[6] I was encouraged to read, read, read. Teachers in this world and the next arrived to help me.

An opportunity to learn tai chi arrived and I experienced the feel of energy moving around my body.[7] The healing energy in my hands became stronger and I also received bursts of Universal Energy[8] in my body, causing me to feel hot. From the initial random arrival of this energy, I discovered I could influence it by my thoughts by either accepting and building on it or consciously choosing not to participate at that moment. Energy – its availability, its use and finally the waves of information it brought – became an increasingly important part of my life, although I am still learning to receive the information with more ease and accuracy. I understood the suggestion to share some of my experiences with others so they might accept the things that were happening to them. All my life I had kept quiet about my experiences, but I now started to talk about them openly with family first, then friends and finally colleagues.

All my life I had kept quiet about my experiences, but I now started to talk about them openly with family first, then friends and finally colleagues.

Finally, I discovered the earliest incarnation in which I questioned the meaning of life and expressed the belief that surely, we are not born, struggle to survive and then die, game over. That would be pointless and irrational. From my closeness to the soil at that time, I knew Mother Nature was many things, but she was not irrational. It was a short but significant life for me as a single man scratching out a livelihood as a farmer

---

5 **Meditation:** The practice of concentrated focus upon a sound, object, visualisation, the breath in order to increase awareness of the present moment. It reduces stress, promotes relaxation and enhances personal and spiritual growth.

6 **Intuition:** A thing that one knows or considers likely from instinctive feeling rather than conscious reasoning. Synonyms include hunch, feeling, feeling in one's bones, gut feeling, inkling, sneaking suspicion, suspicion and impression.

7 **Tai chi:** An ancient Chinese martial art that today is practised as an exercise system that uses slow, smooth body movements to achieve a state of relaxation of body and mind.

8 **Universal Energy:** Also known as universal love or intelligent love, it is the energy that sustains life, providing vital energy to all living systems. A thought is a condensed form of universal mental energy created and directed by a particular entity. Souls sensitive to the universal vibrations are more aware of the energy around them, including the energy of the environment and even that of people who are not related to them. Much information and wisdom can be found within Universal Energy.

in Neolithic Spain. I had incarnated many times before this, but I had not challenged myself to question what life was about.

Having understood the limits of my own conscious lives, my education has moved to the wider universe. In taking the lead from my guide, I read virtually any spiritual books he sent my way. I found a range of books from those based purely on faith and trust, to those which were based on science. The science ones were trying to push the boundaries of our scientific understanding to explain this extraordinary universe we live in. It is good to have both reference points to help you to understand what is happening in your own inner landscape as your conscious awareness evolves.

Humanity Is at a Pivotal Point

Alison: As shown by the amount of conflict in the world, humanity is at a critical point and needs to make changes to enable peaceful and productive living. The requirement to change may be explained by the alteration of the influencing energies from the cosmos as we transition from the Piscean Astrological Age to the Aquarian Age. It is believed that the Piscean Age, which has served us well for over 2,000 years, will come to a close in 2150 and the Aquarian Age will then continue for another 2,160 years. These ages overlap one another by about 200 years, a transition period between the two ages. We are in that transition period today.

In the Aquarian Age it is predicted that the whole of humanity will be uplifted so their consciousness knows, experiences and lives being connected to each other and with Universal love.

In the Aquarian Age it is predicted that the whole of humanity will be uplifted so their consciousness knows, experiences and lives being connected to each other and with Universal love. There is a significant overlap of the two ages, and humanity is experiencing the energies from both ages at the moment. As we move more fully into the Aquarian Age humanity needs to step up on how we treat each other and nature. Increasingly we are seeing the burning ground for change. We experienced the Covid pandemic of 2020, which created much uncertainty and fear. You have only to listen to the news to hear of ongoing issues of war, violence and economic hardship to appreciate an increasing pressure to change how we live. All of these situations test how we choose to behave as an individual, country and species. Many have yet to realise we are all one and how we treat others in turn affects how others treat us.

I believe the needed change in humanity starts with ourselves. We can consciously choose how we lead our life and strive to be the best we can. This can simply be choosing to live by particular life values such as honesty, listening, and caring for others. It isn't as easy as you might think, as I found when I tried to be totally honest in all I said and did. As I listened to myself, I found I was making mistakes and had to correct myself. For example, total honesty includes such things as how you fill out your tax return. Being grateful for your income, I believe, includes paying the right taxes to contribute to the society you live in.

I belive the needed change in humanity starts with ourselves.

As each of us makes higher choices in our lives so the changes will ripple across the peoples of the world. I am starting to see this happen and believe it will be our political and economic leaders who will need to catch up. The esoteric wisdom predicts new discoveries, one of which is in energy – how we get it and use it to assist humanity to live more respectfully of their impact on the planet we call home. What an impact on our lives and surroundings just this change would make! But others are predicted as well.

Andrea Learnt to Make Sense of the Experiences of Her Outer and Inner Worlds

Alison: My observation of Andrea is that she has relentlessly followed her intuition. Her psychic mediumship training helped, but much of her spiritual development was a solitary journey. I like to think of your intuition as a beacon that can send and receive messages to your guides, passed loved ones and finally, with clarity, to your own soul – that divine spark which resides in all of us. From childhood Andrea spoke with her soul but didn't recognise who it was. As she developed, she thought she was talking to a spirit guide. Finally, she came to realise it was her own soul.

As Andrea learnt to converse with her soul more easily, she was able to blend her inner and outer landscapes. She often sought guidance in everyday situations to help her to make the best decisions and to behave with compassion to others and herself. It was a gradual process but has become very much a part of who she is now.

Finding the Courage to Express Your Spiritual Beliefs and Capabilities

Andrea: Being unexpectedly widowed in my forties was a pivotal point in my life. One day I woke up with a husband beside me. I went to bed alone. He was gone and I was alone with the responsibility of raising our two children. I did have my mum for a while, but she passed eighteen months later to the day after my husband. If it is really true that we plan our lives before we are born, as a project manager in this life it was clear to me that I had done a top-down life plan.[9] My husband was planned to live until he was fifty years old, which is a nice round number. I will need some comfort afterwards, so Mum lives another eighteen months. Then my work on who I really am, my strengths and weaknesses, really began.

I remember the first year after my mum passed as the loneliest and bleakest year of my life. I had started to rebuild my life since widowhood, but it was still early days. My mum had been my greatest supporter on moving my life forwards. She had surprised me on how modern and progressive her views were. Now she was gone too. It was a double blow after losing my husband, and I felt even lower. My motivation to live disappeared, and I was glad of the demands of being a parent to get me out of bed in the morning. I wasn't sleeping well. No matter how tired I was when I went to bed, I woke at 2 a.m. and couldn't go to sleep again. I just lay there wondering what I was going to do with the rest of my life and if I would ever experience joy again. It was in one of my early morning reflections that I stumbled on going within. In my inner landscape I didn't find more chaos and anguish but a place of calmness

In my inner landscape I didn't find more chaos and anguish but a place of calmness where I found love, strength and wisdom.

9 **Top-down life plan:** This plan starts from a high level of detail but does not always address the lower levels of detail.

where I found love, strength and wisdom. I didn't then appreciate or understand what I was doing but I did feel comforted, along with gaining greater resolve to live my life.

Widowhood certainly turbo-charged my spiritual development. However, I have always had a curiosity in spiritual matters. I had been highly involved with our local church in my youth and graduated to being a Sunday school teacher. Dad was worried that I was going to become a nun and actively encouraged me to go out with boys. Not many dads do that, but I came to realise why when I understood the longer horizon of my lives and the mistakes I had made in them.

In the months and years after visiting my inner landscape for the first time, I read every spiritual book that crossed my path. I seemed to be guided, and doors opened for me as I moved from books to workshops to training as a psychic medium. For many years I was a closet medium and never spoke of it outside very close friends and my medium friends. I found the training therapeutic through healing meditations, learning to consciously go within and to explore my inner landscape and meet my guides. Finally, I met my own soul and experienced a great love affair.

The marvels of psychic medium training are to discover how supported you are on your life's journey.

The marvels of psychic medium training are to discover how supported you are on your life's journey. I never received a single negative message and always found my guidance uplifting. That is not to say it wasn't challenging, as I was guided to lead a better life through examining and consciously choosing my life values. The real value to me of the psychic mediumship training was to learn the language of my soul and guides.

I had no desire to be a professional psychic medium, but I found many benefits in sitting in a psychic medium circle. I have met some wonderful people who were appreciative of the challenges in my life but encouraged me to find ways of managing myself and my life to overcome them. It was that encouragement which has led me to find my courage to share my story of a wider timeline of lives and learning – what James Redfield in *The Celestine Vision* calls 'the longer now'.

Alison: The story in this book is how Andrea followed her intuition to guide her on the path of spiritual awakening and how it impacted on her family and friends. She was able to access information, learning and hopefully wisdom from a wider time horizon to help her with everyday life and relationships in this lifetime. It wasn't something she did in a class or a workshop, but she absorbed the wisdom into her being and used it to negotiate the challenges of relationships and difficult situations.

The story in this book is how Andrea followed her intuition to guide her on the path of spiritual awakening and how it impacted on her family and friends.

Sometimes she didn't realise what was happening to her, so she read may different spiritual books to understand the contexts of what was happening to her body and her mind in this lifetime. At times she thought perhaps she was going insane, but at the same time she had both a sense of purpose and inner peace.

Wherever you are on the path of spiritual awakening, and if you are reading this book you are probably on the path already, the aim of sharing Andrea's story is to help you to understand your own experiences so they have more meaning to you. However, do try to remember that this is a marathon and not a sprint. The value to you comes from the journey rather than the objective of enlightenment. It is a journey to be enjoyed rather than to be rushed, as there are truly some wonderful joys along the way.

An Aid to Discovering Yourself

Each of you is following your own journey. To help you to appreciate Andrea's journey and thereby aid you on your own journey, Andrea's story and its learnings have been have been broken into three parts:

1. **Past Lives Remembered** gives short accounts of these past lives and what was learnt in them. These have been grouped into three periods in time: the Ancient World, the Middle Ages and the Modern World.
2. **The Wider View of Spiritual Development** explains human physiology, a simple model for spiritual development, and the more

detailed Esoteric Wisdom structure for spiritual development, and provides guidance on how you might understand yourself better and learn to create a better version of yourself.

3. **What Can Humanity Look Forward To?** is a discussion on whether humanity can achieve uplifting ourselves into a better way of being, the platform for change, prophesies for the 21st century, practices to aid living your best life and awakening your soul, your soul type, and the question of death.

In all of this, please remember each of us is on our own personal journey but there are many similarities across our life lessons, life values and the ways of moving our own life forwards. We are simply offering you the knowledge of Andrea's journey, and an analysis of how her experiences, learnings, successes and failures have made her the person she is today to help you on your own journey. Andrea and I have undertaken research, tried different techniques and learnt the hard way through trial and error to discover what felt both helpful and useful. In Parts 2 and 3 we share the results of that work with you with the intent of trying to make your journey easier, more understandable and more fulfilling.

Each of us is on our own personal journey, but there are many similarities across our life lessons and life values.

Perhaps our favourite approach to moving your life forwards are the seven practices for aiding you to live your best life. They help you to awaken your awareness of your soul and to letting it into your life. Each practice is very simple:

1. Step back and observe yourself.
2. Respond rather than react.
3. Follow your passions.
4. Be part of the change in humanity.
5. Consciously choose the life values you wish to live by.
6. What gifts have you inherited from your blood line and culture?
7. Keep going and don't give up.

These are outlined in more detail in Part 3. But remember: do only what feels right for you.

Part 1

Past Lives Remembered

Chapter 1: Past Lives Remembered

Many of our emotional reactions to individuals, plus illnesses and phobias, relate to experiences in past lives. Understanding our past lives thus helps us to understand ourselves. Lessons which have been hard to learn are reinforced when we remember our lives. Additionally, issues caused by different challenges in past lives seem to fade when we remember the experience. There are many techniques for remembering past lives, and you can research and choose the right one for you. Andrea found that working with Soul Maps and painting her personal mandala aided remembering her soul family, who was in it and what they were helping her to learn. She found it facilitated the veil lifting and being able to remember the experiences, knowledge and love gained over the millennia in many different lives.[10]

Andrea found that working with Soul Maps and painting her personal mandala aided remembering her soul family.

Andrea: Let me share a few of my experiences in this life that were caused by past life experiences, to aid your understanding.

In my current life, aged seventeen, I met my late husband at a dance in Oxshott village hall. From the first dance I had with him, I was very attracted to him and knew he would be important to me. We related to

10 **Veil:** Something which hides or covers something or someone. In the spiritual context the veil signifies the veil of ignorance which keeps the knowledge hidden. As you are born into each life you cannot consciously remember previous lives and the wisdom learnt. The challenge is to lift yourself above the veil to remember who you really are.

each other as partners in life, and we were married for nearly twenty-five years before he passed. We have as well spent other lives together in partnership.

By the time I was forty-seven, life had thrown me some challenges and I had become much more cautious. However, the first time my current husband and I danced and we looked in each other's eyes, we recognised one another from past lives. Although he is an accountant by profession and risk averse by nature, within two weeks he had proposed and I had accepted. We had a mutual agreement between us, but it was many months before we told our respective families.

When our families met, almost straight away there was a special relationship between my daughter and my new father-in-law. My husband 'to be' found it difficult to understand how such a deep relationship could develop so quickly. However, this was explained when it became apparent that in a previous life together, my father-in-law had been my daughter's home tutor and was much loved. The relationship he had with my daughter was special from the moment in that life when he held her, just after she was born, and she was no bigger than the palm of his hand. Since then, he has always felt very protective of her and this has rippled across 2,500 years to this life.

The relationship he had with my daughter was special from the moment in that past life when he held her, just after she was born.

In a life in ancient Egypt, I experienced the Romans invading and conquering our country. They brought a new culture and religion which we were forced to adopt. I resented being controlled and as a result I have brought into this life a need not to be controlled. By contrast, my husband has experienced in past lives losing his family as a child through pogroms and dying alone in his World War I life, resulting in him trying to control his family to keep them close to him. These contrasting needs cause us to clash sometimes. Perhaps by understanding our needs in some way I could ease their impact.

In this life I have been severely asthmatic since I was a baby. It relates back to several lives where I was a nun and gave a great deal but received nothing back; in fact, I had come to expect to give and not to receive. This created an imbalance in my energies. In this life in my middle years, I have learnt to receive. This was crystallised while I was reading *Reconnective Healing* by Eric Pearl when I learnt to reconnect to the Universal Energy available to us all. I now no longer carry asthmatic ventilators or medicine, something I would never have dreamt of doing previously. I would panic if they were not at hand in case I had an asthma attack. I have now successfully travelled halfway round the world, to Hong Kong and China, without my asthma drugs and not given it a thought.

> ***Once I remembered my first past life, the others have tumbled out over time.***

Similarly, I have always been claustrophobic in this life. This related back to a Cathar life where I suffocated from being bricked up in a cave. Once I remembered this life, the symptoms disappeared and I could undertake a full body scan in a very claustrophobic tube with no undue stress.

My Greek Hellenistic life is very linked to this current life. That life did not go to plan and much karma was created. I have been able to remember this Greek life to help the participants overcome that karma in this life, something we are all still working on.

What I have found is that once I remembered my first past life, the others have tumbled out over time as it became important in this life for me to remember them. It's as if the memory of a past life contains two reminders:

1. A reminder of a lesson to be learnt and an aid to learning that lesson.
2. A reminder of a lesson or skill learnt in a past life which would help me in my current life.

In this book I have catalogued my past lives I can remember at the time of writing, and the lessons I believe that relate to them, either learnt or to be learnt. For me there appear to be repeating themes of learning to improve communication, accepting that being joyful is good, testing boundaries by being an early adopter of the new technology of that age, and trying to understand the purpose of life by sampling many different religions. In a number of lives going back as far as ancient Egypt I have remembered how to connect to Spirit but then promptly forgotten it in the next life! Developing my capabilities has been a challenge as I keep going back to the beginning – perhaps in this life with the memory of former lives I will have the confidence in myself to be able to move forward.

Alison: In researching the times and cultures of Andrea's past lives. I have noticed that life values which are considered good and behaviours that are acceptable change over time. As Andrea's husband reminded her, as a European psychic medium in the 1500s she would have been burnt as a witch!

Life values which are considered good and behaviours that are acceptable change over time.

In taking a helicopter view of Western history, we can see that there have been three ancient civilisations, the Egyptians, Greeks and Romans, which have strongly influenced the Western world. This led to the emergence of Judaism, Christianity in various forms and Islam, which continue to interplay in our modern world today as national boundaries weaken. As world travel becomes easier and cheaper, individuals gain a greater appreciation of different countries and cultures in terms of food, clothes, and music, which begin to blend. However, many individuals hold strong beliefs in their own religions, which can result in sharp differences in views and attitudes.

For convenience, I have broken our history down into three periods across which Andrea's lives are lived:

- The Ancient World
- The Middle Ages
- The Modern World

To help you to appreciate acceptable behaviours of the time, there is a diagram for each period annotated with key global events against which Andrea's lives are mapped, plus a brief introduction to the period.

Andrea: Alison took a logical approach to appreciating our global history. I took a more intuitive one, working with my main guide, Wang, who comes to me as a Tibetan monk who has a great sense of humour.

Education in the UK teaches national history and the key highlights of major world civilisations. However, most times it does not give a holistic view of world history and how it interacts and overlaps across the world. Fortunately, I have a great love of history and Wang set out to broaden my education. I can remember important historical events, but as a dyslexic I struggle to remember the detail. Understanding the political and social backdrop to my lives was important to appreciate their meaning. Learning and researching the detail of a worldview also seemed to assist me in remembering additional lives.

This summary gives you a perspective of world history rather than a national one.

Wang's sessions, where information was streamed to me, often happened in the middle of the night. I can only assume that I was more receptive to the connection during my sleep. It would then reach a pitch where I would wake up and reach for my iPad to substantiate and verify the information I was being given. Wang loves my iPad and uses it to guide me to information. It's much easier for me to read the detail of a topic on my iPad than have to listen really hard to obtain the information. After a couple of hours, I would end up with numerous tabs open at the top of my screen and a much broader appreciation of how human political and social history has evolved. I would then happily go back to bed and in the morning return to the tabs and note the key facts I had learnt.

Much information was conveyed to me, but below Alison and I have attempted to provide a summary of this information to give you a perspective of world history rather than a national one. However, I have to say that to date the lives I can remember cover a geographical spread from America to the UK to Europe to the Middle East. At this moment in time, I have no conscious memory of lives in India or China so I have limited my world view from America to the Middle East. I am sure I have had lives in the Far East, but they are just not relevant at this moment in time with where I am in this life. I am sure this will change over time. In fact, I have had a flicker of a memory of a life in India with two good girlfriends I have currently in this life. I was given a flash of a memory where my two friends and I were young girls living in northern India. We were wearing beautiful highly coloured saris, had our heads together in conversation and were laughing and twirling our dresses.

Much of my professional life involves working in teams where I am the only woman. Currently I am being reminded that I should not forget to nurture the feminine side of me and to remember to have some fun with girlie laughter, clothes and chatter.

Multiple Lives Prior to Awakening

Andrea: I lived many lives prior to my awakening to the presence of a spiritual spark deep within me. For these lives, I do not remember any particular significant moments for my development. The memories are like the blur of a video showing many everyday moments but with no thread of learning pulling them together. They are simple impressions rather than having any intelligent analysis applied to them. Such as they are, here are the impressions I remember.

There were great forests in a number of lives. These were ancient forests with many different species of trees. They weren't cultivated woods as we see now in much of our countryside. When a tree died, it stayed where it fell. I came to appreciate that a friendly forest would protect and feed you if you respected it and the Spirit of the Forest.

I remember moving in and out of the forests in a number of different bodies, the earliest of which was short, dark and very hairy. I can't remember much about the detail of these lives or any significant learnings. I was fairly simple and just got through each life – and they were sometimes quite violent – without any expectation of improving how I lived.

I was able to see and interact with elves and gnomes. (The elves were quite mischievous.) Although this ability faded, my soul has always remained close to nature and all who live in it. Recently I have regained my ability to see and interact with the Spirit of the Forest near my home. As I develop and my perceptions expand, I have wondered if I have gone full circle.

Chapter 2: The Ancient World

The ancient period takes us from the times of humans being hunter-gatherers, with only mythology informing us of their lifestyle, to the end of the Roman period in 325 CE. The diagram on the next page shows the overlapping periods of the ancient Pharaohs with ancient Greece, the period where Egypt was ruled by the Greek Ptolemy dynasty, which in itself overlaps with the Romans, with Egypt being eventually conquered by the Roman Emperor Octavian. The last 300 years of this period sees the split between Rome and the Jews, and the appointment of the first Latin Pope.

The Ancient World: Andrea's Lives

Humanity moved from being hunter-gatherers to an agriculture-based society, and we saw the development of the key ancient cultures in the West – Egyptian, Greek and Roman. It is against this backdrop that Andrea had a life in a farming community which primed her to question the meaning of her own existence. Andrea first questioned the meaning of life as a farmer in Neolithic Spain – a short but very significant life for her.

Having sampled agricultural life, Andrea then moves to ancient Egypt with lives based around the pyramids and new learnings in science. Today she still loves science and new discoveries. Between these lives Andrea sampled the ancient civilisation of Minoa and then the new civilisation of

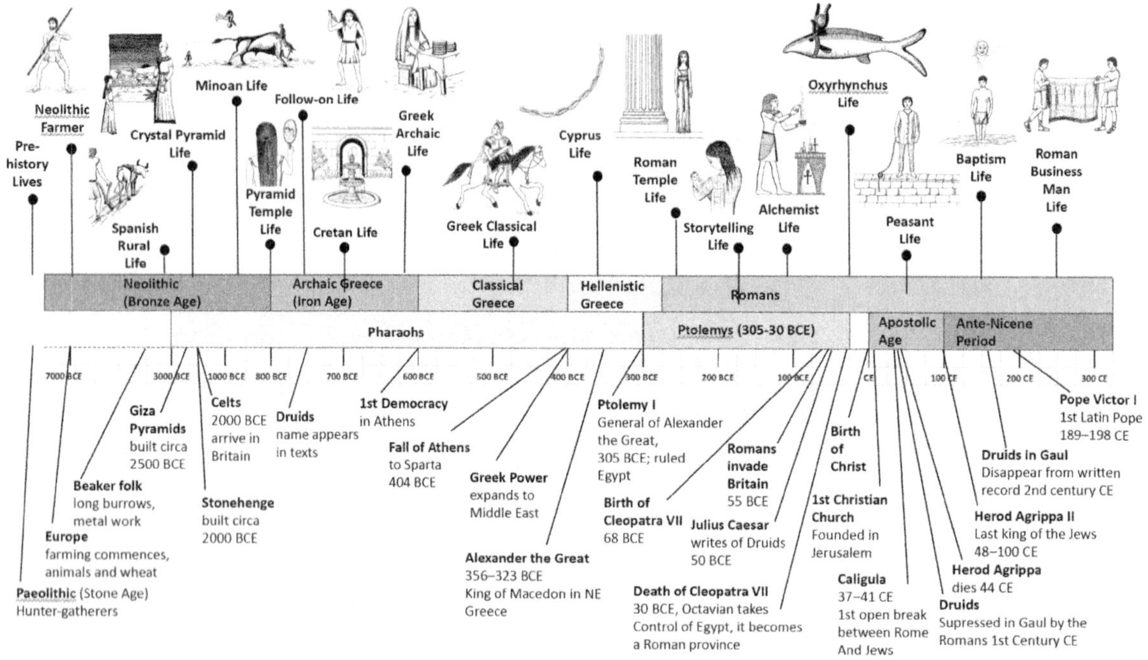

Figure 1: Ancient World Events and Andrea's Lives

Note: The Neolithic and early Pharaonic periods are not to scale.

Greece. As the Romans became more dominant, she again sampled priesthood but this time in a Roman temple. Twice Andrea returns to Egypt before she tries the new religion, Christianity. Finally, she tries out business as an international clothier delivering beautiful and highly coloured robes to the aristocracy of Rome. The materials are sourced from countries across the Roman Empire. Andrea still has the love of business and business skill she first learnt in Roman times.

Key themes in Andrea's lives during the Ancient World period were:

New technology – shoes, and ploughs pulled by animals in Neolithic Spain, healing among the pyramids, reading and writing in Egypt, international trade in Roman times.

Healing and mediumship – in the priesthood associated with the pyramids, Greek temple and story-telling lives.
Religions – a variety of pre-Christian religions, and early Roman Christianity.
Invasion – experienced the Romans invading Egypt and the forcing of their lifestyle on the conquered people. This started Andrea's need not to be controlled.

Andrea's neolithic farmer's life 5,000 years ago was a pivotal moment in her development. She caught a brief glimpse of her own soul.

We have come to appreciate that Andrea's neolithic farmer's life 5,000 years ago was a pivotal moment in her development. It was the first time she consciously questioned the meaning of life and caught a brief glimpse of her own soul. In the EsotericWisdom, it is known as the Awakening and is the start of her long journey to uplift her soul and its consciousness to appreciate who she really is and the wider reality of life. This is where Andrea's story begins.

The Ancient World: Move from Hunter-Gatherers

Around 7,000 BCE humans moved around in family groups hunting and gathering their food. They had implements which were made of stone, leading to this period being called the Stone Age. The Neolithic period saw humans ceasing to roam the countryside for food and commencing farming of animals and the growing of wheat. The start of the Neolithic period occurred over an extended period commencing in the warmer Mediterranean area and spreading northwest across Europe. With a more stable food supply we start to have more available time to construct beautiful objects in bronze and to build long barrows for our dead leaders. Stonehenge is built in England circa 2000 BCE.

Neolithic Farmer: Before Awakening to Who I Am

Andrea: As a young neolithic farmer coming into adulthood, I was in my adolescence and just starting to find girls. I still spent most of my time with other young men, but we were trying to engage with women in the hopes of gaining a partner. I had a large frame and fair hair. My best friend was smaller, slighter of frame and had dark hair. We had been friends from as early as we could remember. He was keener to chase women than I was, but we still enjoyed chasing rabbits, rough-and-tumbling in the dirt together and running free across the uplands. My friend was sharper witted than me and liked to win in our games. We were like opposites who fitted together to make a whole. He was dark, short and competitive whereas I was fair, tall and easy-going.

We had recently been given staves as we came into manhood. They were new to us and we were proud to carry them. We used them to help us with herding the sheep, and as assistance when we walked long distances to the further edges of our farm. Ultimately, we could use them for defence should we encounter trouble away from the homestead.

My friend and I were attracted to the same girl. We could not agree who should try to win her, so we decided to have a fistfight over her. Being larger I was winning the fight and in the heat of the moment, my friend grabbed his staff, swung it above his head and hit my hip. I was powerless to protect myself and my hip made an ominous noise. In those times, a broken hip could be fatal. If you couldn't work you didn't eat, and you certainly didn't have a partner and a family.

The moment the staff hit my hip, the woman who had been indifferent to both of us fell in love with me. She took me into her family home and nursed me back to health. When I was able to walk again, albeit with a significant limp, I was able to work and could claim this woman as my own. We successfully raised three children and were a happy family, but for the rest of that life I was always in pain, something that spoilt what could have been a good life.

I felt betrayed by my friend, so we never spoke again. He was disgraced in our village and was not treated very kindly. However, I still missed him and I mourned for the loss of our friendship, which had run so deep.

This life taught me in a harsh way that competitiveness and jealousy can lead to betrayal and someone doing things outside of their normal behaviour. When we're almost blinded by the desire to win, we can resort to violent acts without thought of the other person or the consequences. Sadly, once done it cannot be undone.

This experience drove me to wanting to find a better way of living. It became the precursor to another life in which I considered if there was more to life than living a life and dying. So this life, although painful, had a good outcome in the end when you look at a longer time horizon.

Spanish Rural Life: Single Man, and My Awakening

As a neolithic farmer in Spain near Gaudix, to the east of Granada in the *trogloditas* area, I first came to question the purpose of life. Unusually, we used an animal to pull our plough and we wore primitive shoes, both new technologies in their time and which improved our lives.

I can see the back of the animal pulling our primitive plough. The haunches are going up and down as it plods across the field pulling the plough to make a furrow in the ground. It is early spring and the weather has been rainy, making the ground wet and sticky with mud. It takes effort and strength to keep the plough moving straight with the animal plus keeping the animal walking in a straight line. The effort makes me feel hot, but even with shoes my feet feel cold in the soil.

I had a big, sandy-coloured shaggy dog called Snuffles who went everywhere with me, and I adored her. Close to the earth and nature, I knew Mother Nature was structured and orderly and it did not make sense to me that we were born, struggled to survive and then died – game over. It seemed such a waste and most unlike Nature, which constantly regenerated itself with the changing of the seasons. I felt there had to be more to life. Once I had that awakening to the possibility of a different reality, the purpose of that life was achieved and I died young, from being struck from behind with a stick. It always amuses me how my soul never wastes energy and time once a goal has been achieved.

Lessons

Although this was a short life it was a significant life for me and began my Awakening to my soul and stepping onto the path of spiritual development. I had lived many lives before but in those lives, I had just accepted the life I was given and got on with it. It was in this life for the first time I questioned my own reality and asked if there was something more. It was a fleeting expression of my own soul but momentous for my development in learning who I am.

I believe making a start on a journey like this is the hardest thing to do. The first step in any change is the most difficult. I have seen this in my career, where I was involved in implementing business change with new processes, organisations and IT systems. It was no different in Neolithic times – change is challenging, but little step by little step you make change happen. Or perhaps it's lifetime by lifetime; each change for the better may be in small increments but eventually you will look back and see how far you have come. A new way of living can feel strange at first, but when you repeat it many times it becomes comfortable and then almost instinctual.

Once you start this journey, new doors open to help you to move forwards.

I have found that once you start, new doors open to help you to move forwards, whether you do it consciously or subconsciously. The overriding lesson from this life was:

There is purpose to being born and experiencing a life.

Change is challenging but it can bring great satisfaction. You can stay in one state in how you live and behave. To move forwards and progress takes effort. But personally, I find that effort rewarding as you gain a greater sense of yourself, understand ways to be your best self and learn to appreciate the wider reality in which you live.

So I set out on my journey in Neolithic times, some 5,000 years ago. As I share with you my lives and experiences, I will outline the life lessons I have been learning to gain my personal wisdom. Things don't always go to plan, but I have found that humour eases the tension of failure, enabling me to find the strength to try again.

'Allow yourself to believe in your ability and it will arrive.'
– Eric Pearl, author of *The Reconnection: Heal Others, Heal Yourself*

Andrea: As if to emphasise the significance of this life to my development, my soul, through my husband and wonderful soul travel guide, took me back to the location of this neolithic life in southern Spain. Before our holiday I had known a significant event would happen and felt compelled to draw a picture of a valley with cliffs and homes built into them.

It was in this valley that I had been ploughing when I caught the first glimpse of my soul.

As we drove towards the city of Guadix we entered a broad valley with hills on either side. It was in this valley that I had been ploughing when I caught the first glimpse of my soul. It was here that is the true beginning of my story. I just couldn't draw my eyes away from the flat plains of that valley, but at that moment I didn't know why.

The scene felt familiar, but I couldn't place it. I didn't know the significance of the picture I had drawn until we were on the outskirts of Guadix and you could see the cave homes, the valley and the hills together in the same configuration as my picture. History tells us that the Guadix caves were first developed when Catholic kings took over the Moorish city in 1489. The Moors moved to the outskirts of the city and dug into the red clay that lines the hills to create homes within them. However, I have a memory of such homes in the same area but in Neolithic times. They were not as large and elaborate as those now in Guadix, but the principle of making use of the clay hills for shelter was the same.

The Ancient World: Druid Religion

The Druid religion establishes itself and appears in language and written text. The Romans first invade Britain in 55 BCE, and in 50 BCE Julius Caesar during one of his campaigns writes of the Druids. However, the Druids are challenged by the Romans. They are suppressed in Gaul and disappear from the written record by the 2nd century CE. There is one last written reference to the Druids in a poem in 750 CE.

Andrea: I can't remember any explicit lives during this time. However, I do remember reading about the churches in the counties of Somerset and Dorset in the UK where my family come from, which were historically Druid centres. Druids regarded hilltops as sacred areas, as they used them to view the rising and setting of the sun. When the Druid religion was being suppressed, these sacred areas were used by Christians to build their churches.

My great-great-grandad was strong, forceful and loud; nothing had changed much for him for being in the After Life.

My great-great-grandad was a master mason and cycled or walked to many of these churches for work. He is a character in our family and was still spoken of when I was a child. We are a family of healers and mediums, a skill absorbed from the old religions and handed down the generations to today. I was made aware of this in a sitting with a medium in which my great-great-grandad came to visit me. His character was much as my family had described him. When the medium could not quite get his name right, he shouted it at us so loud it bounced around the walls of my mind. He was strong, forceful and loud. It made me smile; nothing had changed much for him for being in the After Life.

The Ancient World: Egyptian Pharaohs and the Rise of Greek Power

While much of Europe is still in the Neolithic period of early farming, the Egyptians have developed a more sophisticated culture. The great pyramid of Giza is believed to have been built 2560 to 2540 BCE, there is written language, science has commenced and society is organised. This continues for many hundreds of years.

We see the rise of Greek culture from 800 BCE. Greek philosophy develops in the 6th century BCE, leading to well-known philosophers such as Socrates, Plato and Aristotle. The first democracy is established in Athens in the 6th century BCE. Learning expands in the Greek Hellenistic and Roman periods. Many different schools of thought developed with contributions from the Greeks, Romans, Egyptians, Syrians and Arabs

Athens falls to Sparta in 404 BCE and Greek power shifts eastwards, first to Thebes and then Macedonia. Alexander the Great, king of Macedonia, builds the largest empire in the ancient world. It spreads from the Ionian Sea to the Himalayas. His general Ptolemy takes charge of Egypt in 305 BCE and Ptolemy's family rules the country until the death of Cleopatra in 30 BCE.

Ancient Egypt, Crystal Pyramid Life: Young Girl, Keeper of the Light

As a young girl, six or seven years old, I climbed with a man to an aperture high on a pyramid where we looked out across the land. It was warm and pleasant, early in the evening when the work of the day is done and everyone is looking forward to the meal of the evening. Family groups were gathering outside their homes. Although the sun was setting and it was getting dark, there was a warm yellow light around the houses. Food was being cooked even though there were no visible signs of smoke.

With great love the man who accompanied me explained to me the importance of knowledge and how it might help to keep the people and land we loved, well and healthy. He placed a small crystal pyramid in my left hand and my hand became warm.

I have had a similar experience in this lifetime when I was choosing a crystal skull. It is as if the crystal chooses you rather than the other way around. When I picked up a rose quartz skull and placed it on my left palm it went warm, just as the crystal pyramid had done all those years ago.

Learning how to raise your personal energy to be able to link with Universal Energy and Mother Earth's electromagnetic energy was part of the training to become the Keeper of the Light. This girl and her colleagues learnt how to give energy healing as part of their own spiritual journey. Offering healing was very much part of the activities of the priesthood associated with the pyramids.

I had chosen before birth to become the 'Keeper of the Light' to challenge my capabilities to connect while in a body.

I sensed, rather than being explicitly told, that this man was leaving us. His role in the priesthood was being passed to me. He was worried because I was so young and had been given so little time to absorb the knowledge of how to provide light and heat to our people. It is a knowledge which was passed down through the generations but can only be used if it comes with both humility and wisdom. The wisdom is learnt over many lifetimes. This girl had that wisdom, but could she lift her consciousness sufficiently above the veil while living in a body to remember it?

The love I felt from this man I have only experienced in this lifetime during a near-death experience during childhood. The person receiving me into the After Life and questioning me on whether I wanted to pass radiated the same all-consuming love. There was no judgement on what I chose to do. All decisions were right, even if some of them would give me more of a challenge than others. I felt free to choose without recrimination. And so, in this ancient Egyptian life, I had chosen before birth to become the 'Keeper of the Light' at a very tender age to challenge my capabilities to connect while in a body. In this respect, it wasn't a great success, as on my watch the light of ancient Egypt went out and the rulers took the pyramids as their own. They subjugated their own people rather than sharing the healing and energy the pyramids had to offer.

Lessons

Failures in a life seem to be rebalanced by trying again in another life. This brings about the balance in my own energy and the energy of those I have affected a previous failure. It is a slightly different view of karma from the traditional one.[11] For me, it isn't about punishment for failure but balance when you succeed in a capability or skill and is therefore something to be celebrated. From this lifetime I still remember and feel:

- *Knowledge imparted with love is remembered with love.*
- *If you don't succeed the first time, try and try again until you do.*
- *Sharing wisdom such as the ability to heal should be given generously without personal gain.*

This ancient Egyptian life and the fading of the knowledge to provide clean, available and free energy resonates strongly with my current life.

This ancient Egyptian life and the fading of the knowledge to provide clean, available and free energy resonates strongly with my current life. I feel there is more work to be done to balance out that failure in ancient Egyptian times. This Egyptian life was about knowingly connecting with Universal Energy through raising your conscious awareness and using it for healing and the sharing of wisdom. My quest today in this life is very similar.

I studied psychic mediumship to learn the language of my soul and guides. I learnt to reconnect with Universal Energy through reading Eric Pearl's book *The Reconnection: Heal Others, Heal Yourself.* My hands came alive with energy. I experimented with it, starting with my cut flowers in my home – and I had amazing results. I was grateful that my having cut flowers to enjoy in my home didn't impact their lives so much. I started to see the glow of energy around the flowers, something I had intuitively felt and enjoyed before I was able to apply the energy in my hands to them.

I feel experiencing energy in your body with the ability to heal others can be part of your own spiritual journey. To extend my experience, I learnt and practiced reiki for some time. The offering of healing energy morphed from reiki into a more general energy healing, where I call in the client's guide and my guides. Sometimes I include the use of a crystal as well. It was at this point that the 2020 pandemic struck and I moved

11 **Karma:** In the law of 'cause and effect', karma is the cause of your actions – mental, vocal and physical – which generate an effect. The belief is that whatever you do comes back to you – for example, if you do something good, something good will happen to you, and vice versa.

my healing sessions to being online. The client and I chatted and saw each other as usual. Then the client would lie down on their bed and I visualised them in front of me and gave them a normal healing session. I discovered that indeed distance has no effect on energy. It works even if the healer and their patient are on opposite sides of the world. It is truly amazing.

I feel healing energy should be freely given to anyone who desires it. Perhaps this desire comes from a principle I learnt as part of my Crystal Pyramid life.

I feel healing energy should be freely given to anyone who desires it.

> *'When I was going through treatment for cancer, I found it comforting to have a weekly energy healing session with Andrea. I felt it was good for my health and eased the side effects of the treatment. As Andrea is a psychic medium, there was the added benefit of messages of support and love from my mum and dad, who have passed. Sessions with Andrea were uplifting and I came away feeling better.'*
>
> – Doris, Camberley, Berkshire

This is what my friend, a retired anaesthesiologist, has shared on his views on healing:

> *'I have a strong belief that a blend of Western and alternative healing achieves the best outcome with overcoming poor health. Personally, I try energy healing first and have had some success in healing a knee ailment and therefore avoiding a painful operation. For critically ill patients such as those with cancer, my observation over the course of my career is that a blend of Western medicine and alternative healing gives the best result. Care is needed to ensure that Western medicine does not conflict particularly with herbal and homeopathy treatments.'*
>
> – Helmut, Munich, Germany

A Japanese friend has these views on the value of Eastern medicine and managing your health:

'Like our friend Helmut, I have a strong belief in natural healing. I am Japanese although I have lived in London for over forty years. I have successfully maintained my health through a good lifestyle of diet, exercise and meditation for calmness and inner peace. Should I have a health complaint, I use Eastern medicine as practiced in Japan. I find it works well for my body.'

– Suzy, London, formerly of Nagoya City, Japan

It was at the time of expanding my healing capabilities from reiki to energy that a good friend told me she was terminally ill. The healing I was able to offer her was never going to make her well, but I hoped it would help her emotionally and enable her to enjoy rather than endure the time left to her. These were Fran's thoughts:

'I am living with cancer and know I will never be free of it in this lifetime. This experience has set me on a spiritual journey. When Andrea gives me reiki, It's the only time I truly feel at peace. Thank you, Andrea, for this gift.'

– Permission to use the quote given by her daughter, Alice

Unusually, Fran connected with me in my sleep the day after she passed. This connection came so soon that I wasn't expecting it. She told me that the energy healing enabled her to connect more strongly with her loved ones in the After Life before she passed. Now she is in the After Life, she is able to connect more easily with her children on Earth. The healing helped her to build a stronger bridge so they could all feel more connected. I did wonder if this message was a figment of my imagination. But just before she left, Fran said, *'Until we meet again.'* And gave me a hug. That gesture was so Fran, you couldn't mistake her. I had been greatly affected by her illness and passing. It was so like Fran to console others.

Minoan Life: Boy, Bull Acrobat

As a boy, thirteen or fourteen years old in Minoan Crete, I was slim and athletic. I had been trained from an early age to leap across bulls' backs and participated in festivals giving displays with my fellow leapers. When we were young, we started with leaping across static wooden structures and then graduated to moving animals and finally to the bull. It took great practise to achieve a graceful bull leap and required enormous concentration and focus. Undertaking the feat was dangerous, but I loved the excitement of it. We put a white powder on our hands to help prevent slipping on the bull's back.

My great friend in this work is the soul that is my son in my current life. He still retains the mischievous humour he had in Minoan times. We used to tumble together in a very synchronised way, rather like Ying and Yang energy. In Minoan times my friend had a younger brother who wanted to join in with us practising but was too young and small to cope with the leaps. This small boy wanted to hang onto the bull's tail so he could join in. He definitely did not want to let go. We were not very kind to him and shooed him away. He looked very sad and lonely when we did this. My friend and I had learned how to achieve balance and harmony together, but by totally excluding the little boy we showed that we had not learnt how to achieve a wider balance.

In this life, my friend and his younger brother were boyfriend and girlfriend for a while. It gave my friend the opportunity to learn how to create harmony in a relationship. If a relationship is not right, creating disharmony to make the person walk away is not the right way to go about it.

Lessons

The loneliness my friend's little brother felt has reverberated in my current life. I have always had a fear of being lonely and experienced intense loneliness when both my husband and mother passed. I still struggle with handling being alone. Going within and knowing my inner landscape, especially my soul, has helped me to learn to manage myself better and to know we are never truly alone. The lessons I started to learn in this Minoan life and continue to practise are:

- *Focus, concentration and practise enable us to achieve amazing things.*
- *We are never truly alone.*
- *There are many kind ways of saying 'No'. We need to find them and practise them.*

Ancient Egyptian Temple Life: Young Woman, Psychic

My current-life stepmother-in-law and I were women in a temple associated with the pyramids. My stepmother-in-law in this ancient Egyptian life was much older than me. I was in adolescence, but she was a full-grown woman in her prime.

We were made to look into mirrors to develop our psychic abilities so we could provide information to the rulers. My stepmother was very spiritual and comforted me in this hard, gruelling work. When I became tired, I struggled to connect with Spirit and to get good-quality messages. It is something I continue to struggle with even today. My lack of ability used to anger the men who managed us and they frightened me. My stepmother was very calm. With this calmness and the strength it brought her, she guided and helped me to be a better psychic.

We were kept separate from society, but the priests sexually abused us and that caused me great anguish. I swore in that life that I would not let men do this to me again.

In my current life I expressed my surprise to my mum at women complaining about men making advances to them at work. I had never had that problem, even though I worked in teams where I was often the only woman. I wondered if men did not find me attractive. Mum laughed and said, 'I don't know what it is about you, but you radiate – Do Not Touch Me! Woe betide the man who tried to touch you when you didn't want it.'

Lessons

From the guidance my stepmother-in-law gave me in this ancient Egyptian lifetime, I learnt much about the interaction between people in difficult situations. To summarise these lessons:

- *A kindness offered at a time of challenge is remembered.*
- *In calmness we find our inner strength.*
- *Challenges often help us to learn a lesson about what we will allow to happen to us.*
- *We might believe we have learnt a lesson, but we often check in a later life if that is really true.*

These are all fundamental lessons in learning how to interact more kindly with other people but also with ourselves. We are an important person in our own life. We need to learn to take care of ourselves no matter what situation we find ourselves in. A small kindness can go a long way.

Ancient Egyptian Temple Follow-on Life: Learning to Keep a Promise

In the next life I was reborn as a girl again. I was tested as to whether I would have the strength to follow through on the promise I had made to myself. A man tried to take advantage of me – and I drew a knife on him to protect myself. I can still hear the noise of the knife sliding out of its sheath. I jumped into the attack position with my feet apart, my hair flying, my eyes flashing, and I hissed like a wildcat. The man was not hurt – but I was not molested either. The man in that life was my current-life son. Even in this life as an adult son, he supports me in challenging times. We have a close and heart-felt relationship.

Lessons

The combination of the last two lives and my mum's comment about me really did persuade me of this truth:

- *A lesson learnt transcends the lives we lead.*

Cretan Life and Oracle: Wife and Mother of a Disabled Child

In this Cretan life my current-life maternal grandfather was my husband. My sister-in-law was my eldest daughter, and I had two other daughters. My eldest daughter was troubled with uncontrollable fits. During a fit she would roll on the ground with her limbs flaying and her eyes rolling. There was nothing I could do other than try to hold her so she didn't hurt herself. I used to also make a 'shshshing' noise with my lips and tongue, which seemed to soothe her. In my current life as we held my dad as he was passing, unexpectedly I made this same noise. I remember wondering where it had come from. I'm not sure if it helped my dad as he passed, but I hope it did.

My husband in this Cretan life was a powerful politician and did not like having a daughter who had fits. It made him feel like he had bred an idiot daughter, which of course wasn't true. I went to the Oracle for help and advice. By this time the ancient mother goddess symbol of the snake was complemented by the dove. Advised by the Oracle, I used drugs to keep my daughter quiet so my husband was not embarrassed by her in public at important events. My husband was not kind to our daughter and in subsequent lives had to work this through.

In this Cretan life, together my husband and I built a beautiful villa which was outstanding in its time, not so much for its size but for the thought that went into the design. It was on a hill overlooking the sea, which provided a panoramic view and cooling breezes in the summer. As the summers were hot, we designed it to have cool areas inside and a fountain in the central courtyard to provide a lovely backdrop to the midday sleep. This was the start of our mutual love of architecture. That love has been expressed in this life, as my grandad designed and built beautiful homes. I have followed in the family tradition by improving and managing good-quality rental homes. For me, homes are places where people can experience their greatest well-being. A well-designed home supports the flow of daily living but also provides quiet private space if it is desired. A garden, no matter how small, or shared, is also of great benefit.

Homes are places where people can experience their greatest well-being.

Lessons

- *We love someone for who they are, not what they are.*
- *Working together to provide mutual support is good.*
- *Beautiful buildings can provide a space of peace and harmony.*
- *Outdoor space enables your energy to relax and extend more easily beyond your body.*

These lessons are all about teamwork and managing yourself for well-being. Working together supporting one another, we are stronger than focusing on our own individual life. Humans are tribe-based, and when harmony is achieved teamwork easily happens and can be very rewarding. My sister-in-law and I remember this lesson to this day. Here is her comment about our family Christmas celebrations together:

> *'When Andrea married into our family in her 40s, we settled into a routine of shared Christmas celebrations, alternating each year who hosted the event. I was surprised how naturally and well we worked as a team. On my year, I organised the overall plan and Andrea was the support team. The following year we reversed the roles. Teamwork made Christmas much easier. When Andrea shared her spiritual views, I wasn't sure what to make of them. It gave me food for thought. I wasn't sure how accepting my husband would be of them.'*
>
> – Susan, Portsmouth, UK

Greek Life, Archaic Period: Abused Wife

I was married to an abusive husband who was easily annoyed, and he used to beat me. My son was my current husband today.

This marriage had not been a love match. Our respective families had decided we should marry. My husband was much older than me and didn't really want to be bothered with a young wife.

I left this abusive husband and took my son with me. In those times this was a courageous act, as wives were meant to do as their husbands told them. Errant wives were often treated harshly to discourage other women from becoming too bold. We left in the middle of the night and crept to a small boat, which took us downriver to the coast. There we transferred to a larger boat and travelled to another country, possibly from Ephesus to the Greek mainland. I used much of my jewellery to pay for our passage. My son was limping as he got on the boat from where his father had hit him. We were fearful of what would happen if he caught us leaving.

My son and I started a new life together. We sold flatbread to make a living, and my son worked with me. We didn't make much money so our life was meagre. However, feeling free to be ourselves was invaluable to us. The quality of our lives free from abuse made the hard work of the day worthwhile.

Our life free from abuse was short-lived, however. We died together holding hands from falling masonry during an earthquake. While it was a short life, in that time we had learnt to value and honour ourselves.

Lessons

The length of a life is not the sole criteria of a worthwhile life. Sometimes quite short lives can be of great value to your own development. The lessons from this life are:

- *It is possible to build a new life even in very difficult circumstances.*
- *Finding the courage to change your life for the better is rewarding.*

- *Leading your life as you want to is true freedom and doing so uplifts your soul.*
- *A mother's desire to protect her child can be strong, enabling her to do courageous acts.*

Greek Life, Classical Period: Young Woman Learning Discretion

I was the daughter of a high-ranking soldier, a general. He wore elaborate Greek armour plates for protection and to mark his rank. I had long hair, which I plaited into strands on both sides of my face and tied back. I was pretty and, unusually for Greece, had bright blue eyes, possibly from my mother's family. I was also psychic. I was my father's favourite daughter, and he had great plans to marry me for political advantage.

My father was planning to conduct a war campaign. Using my psychic abilities, I knew it was a poor plan and doomed to failure. I approached my father and told him it was a bad plan. He was used to being obeyed and was very cross at being challenged, especially by a woman. My father took hold of me meaning only to give me a shake to be quiet. However, his forcefulness got out of hand, my head swung back, hitting a wall, and I died. My father was very sad, as I was his favourite and he had such high hopes for me.

Lessons

This life started to show me the value of good communication, especially when the message conveyed is that someone has got something wrong. Not being too direct is still something I have to watch in myself today. However, I have experienced some good results in business from carefully communicating a difficult message. It is often about praising someone for their efforts while correcting how they did it. My spiritual guide is really good at this, and it is something I aspire to do more consistently.

- *Be more considered in my words.*
- *Learn not to dictate and be too pushy – give people time to assimilate the message.*
- *Learning to uplift another person is good.*

Greek Hellenistic Cyprus Life: Young Woman in Difficult Family Circumstances

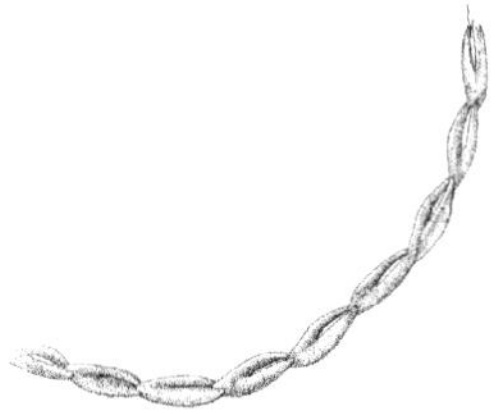

This is the first life I remembered and is very linked to this life. My complete soul family participated in this life. My guide used this ancient Greek life to show me how to use Soul Maps for my development.

This life did not go according to our plan, and much karma was created which we, as a soul family, have spent the last 2,500 years trying to rectify. My current daughter was my sister, my mother was again my mother, my father today was my mother's lover, my son was the son of my mother's lover. My current husband was betrothed to marry me.

Our lives went dramatically wrong, resulting in our house being stormed and my being dragged off and killed. On my funeral bier my fiancée promised to marry me in another life. He had a belief in reincarnation and knew we would meet again and get a chance to rectify our mistakes.

Soon after we met, my current husband gave me a necklace made of silver myrtle leaves. I wear it every day. In ancient Greece a bride wore a crown of myrtle leaves to her wedding. Although an accountant and cautious by nature, in this life my husband proposed within two weeks of us meeting. He did not want to just live together; it was marriage or nothing.

Lessons

This life has been instructive on many levels. It is the life I remember in the most detail. I have even re-experienced some of the scenes from that life to reinforce the learning. It was much as you read about what happens in an After Life review. I'm not sure if this was the result of it being the first life I remembered, or it was the most important life that needed work on, or because I used a Soul Map to explore it. The Soul Map may have helped me to go deeper than on other lives. The key learnings I took from this life are:

- *Love and promises are remembered across lives.*
- *Our actions in one life can influence a future life.*
- *We all make mistakes; it's part of the learning process.*
- *Owning our mistake is the first step to overcoming it.*
- *Our soul family loves and supports us through many lives.*
- *Soul families live in soul communities with community members often represented in our lives.*

We each have to take responsibility for our own karma and to work on it.

The feeling of a strong link from this life to today's life is, I believe, the need to resolve the family karma between soul family members created during that Greek life. Having a knowledge of that Greek life and what went wrong has given me insight into fractious relationships within the family. When someone shows a surprising reaction to something, I now have an appreciation of why they have done this. I have tried to help, but I have not always been successful. We each have to take responsibility for our own karma and to work on it. When opportunities have been missed to resolve difficulties and achieve greater harmony, at least I now know we will get another opportunity in this life or perhaps the next to try again.

Greater family harmony, I feel, is important for my own development. I have a tendency to want to soothe a situation or person, but sometimes it is better to bring things out into the open and discuss them. This can feel like a harder route to take, but it can sometimes achieve a more lasting harmony as it tackles the root cause of conflict rather than the symptoms.

It is a popular belief that your physical ailments come about solely by how you live your current life. However, I believe you may well bring physical weaknesses into this life which are a hangover of physical harm in a previous life. Your soul regards all of your lives as one story, and so is just continuing the story where it was left off in a previous life. Therefore, in a world where many people are right-handed, it is not surprising that there is a predominance of physical weakness in people's left-hand side from former injuries from knives or swords.

In this Greek life I was stabbed in the lower left abdomen and died from loss of blood. With the strong link between this Greek life and today's life to resolve family karma, it is not surprising that throughout my current life I get a pain in this same place if I overdo things. Doctors cannot explain it, as nothing appears to be malfunctioning. It is a weakness that comes to the fore whenever my body feels stressed. Understanding what has caused it has eased the situation, but it has not fully gone away. Perhaps it will when our family are living in harmony.

I have learnt to observe my body for clues to situations which need to be worked on.

From this experience, I have learnt to observe my body for clues to situations which need to be worked on.

The Ancient World: Roman Dominance

As Greek power wanes, Roman power rises. The Romans invade much of Europe, the southern edges of the Mediterranean and as far east as the Caspian Sea, including modern-day Turkey, Georgia and Azerbaijan. Octavian defeats the combined forces of Mark Antony and Cleopatra in a naval engagement at Actium on 2 September 31 BCE, and Octavian takes control of Egypt. Wherever the Romans invade they impose their way of life. The Romans take on much of the learning from Greek culture to blend with their own gods, as well as scientific and philosophical knowledge. To match their political prowess, they seek to dominate the religions of the region.

Following the birth of Christ, the first Christian church is founded in Jerusalem. The reign of Emperor Caligula, 37–41 CE, saw the first open break between Rome and the Jews. Herod Agrippa II is the last king of the Jews. Raised and educated in Rome, Herod Agrippa supports the Romans over his own Jewish people, causing unrest. The Romans appoint their own governor over the Jews. Roman Catholicism continues to spread across the empire, and the first pope is declared in 189 CE, Pope Victor I.

Roman Temple Life: Woman Priestess Forgetting to Look beyond Devotion

I led a devout and spiritual life as a priestess in a Roman temple. I willingly gave up the opportunity for a partner and family to follow my religion. However, I forgot my life mission of sharing spiritual awakening with the wider community. In some ways, although it outwardly looked like a devout and good life, it was actually a rather selfish one, as I focused only on my own spiritual development.

In my current life, I was reminded in my Psychic Mediumship Development Circle of this weakness to go within and ignore my life's mission. It was just as I agreed with Alison to write this book together and I was feeling daunted at tackling the process of going public and getting it published. It brought my attention to that task, as I definitely did not want to fail a second time.

Lessons

- *Life should be balanced, with both families and spiritual development.*
- *Remember to share my spiritual journey with others to encourage them to join me in the journey.*

This failure in ancient Roman times to help others set back my own development. In the temple, I just enjoyed the inner peace of connection to Spirit. I didn't do the work to raise myself above the veil to remember that I was meant to teach others to help them with their spiritual development.

The lesson of blending family life and a spiritual life was a significant one for me. I do have a tendency to be extremely focused when I want to succeed in something, and that blocks my awareness of everything else going on around me. I have learnt the hard way by relationships or lives going wrong that a spiritual life is not meant to be discreet from the rest of your life or from others. It is a way of living and being which is demonstrated in how you behave on a daily basis. Sadly, in subsequent lives I sometimes have forgotten this lesson and had several monastic lives focused solely on learning and connecting with Universal Energy rather than living a fuller life with other people. People can be the most challenging aspect of life, and they therefore bring so many opportunities to learn life lessons. This weakness is highlighted again in my Alchemist life later in Egypt.

The lesson of blending family life and a spiritual life was a significant one for me.

As I mentioned earlier, in my current life my dad was keen for me not to repeat this mistake again. He came into his current life with the task of encouraging me during my growing up to engage in a full adult life with a partner and family and guiding me away from monastic life. As a teenager I became a Sunday school teacher and was greatly involved with our local church. My dad didn't want my interests to grow into a desire to become a nun. So he actively encouraged me to go out with boys to help to awaken me to a wider life and my life's purpose. He wanted me to feel able to follow my soul's desires, but he also wanted me to realise that this did not mean I had to lead a life alone, which could potentially lead to loneliness.

Reflecting on this now, I've thought that perhaps Dad in this life knew more about me than I realised. He appreciated that I needed to work on my family's karma, and that this would be made easier if I had a partner and a family of my own to allow souls to arrive in my life and to love and care for them in my everyday life.

Appreciating what had not worked out for me in this Roman temple life, it is not surprising that my soul chose the following life to help balance my experience.

Storytelling Life: Old Woman in the Roman Empire Guided by Spirit to Care for Others

In this life I had my own babies but in my middle years I took in other peoples' babies when they could not cope with them. In these times of no contraceptives, in the Roman Empire it was common, especially among poorer families, that when a baby was born the father would decide if he accepted it into the family. If he already had plenty of children and didn't feel able to feed another mouth, especially a girl, he could reject the baby. The father would then take the newborn away from its mother and village and leave it naked on the hillside to die. This was the fate of my current-life daughter in these ancient times.

In this life, I loved to be out of doors, away from the village, even though this was against my family's desires. I used to roam far and wide among the hills, and it was on one of those walks that I found this abandoned baby. She was beautiful but I could feel she was already at the point of dying. I picked her up, blessed her and held her until she passed. I was too late to prevent her from dying, but at least I felt that she did not die alone. I didn't want to leave her on the hillside for the crows to peck at her, so I made a rudimentary grave and buried her. This experience started the baby's soul's fear of being left by loved ones. Added to this is a feeling that I am never quite there in time for her, which has bubbled up in her current life.

As this old woman, I started telling stories to the children I helped to raise. Initially I used my imagination, but as I expanded on that capability I started to link with Spirit and messages would be relayed through the stories.

Then I started to tell stories to adults. My reputation grew, and finally I was telling stories to leaders and providing information from Spirit. The leaders wanted readings that would provide them with guidance. My stories were written down, and in working with the scribes I learnt to read and write, which was very unusual for a woman of that time. As I grew old I had long scraggily hair, as I was so interested in what I was doing that I didn't notice how I looked. I could also do channelling and auto-writing.

Lessons

- *I have successfully learnt how to connect to Spirit before.*

Alchemist Life, Egypt: Middle-Aged Man Too Focused on Work

My current-life son was my younger brother in this ancient Egyptian lifetime; my father-in-law from my first husband was my black captor.

I was a very intelligent man studying and working in alchemy in the very early days of the discipline. Unlike today, where alchemy is associated with chemistry, in ancient times it was a blend of mystical and philosophical views and investigating metals such as gold, iron and tin and identifying chemicals. I was smelting ores to extract the metals from them. I was then experimenting with separating the metals and combining them in different ways to create alloys. I still have an interest in science today, and I feel it was my experience in this life that sparked my interest.

What I was doing scared those in power and they locked me up in jail. My younger brother tried very hard to get me released, but the things I said scared the authorities too much, so they refused. I died in jail and my brother was very upset.

Lessons

I was so intent on my work that I didn't consider the impact of going against the ruling authority of the day. Nor did I think about how it would make my loved ones feel if I was incarcerated. While I felt my work was valuable, I was rather selfish in my outlook. My work was everything to me, but my life lacked balance between home and work. This is an age-old lesson that many people are still learning today. I still have a tendency to do this, even now after all these lifetimes. However, I am more self-aware in my current life and when I observe I'm focusing on work too much, I try to address the situation. The key lessons for me were:

- *Communicating in the right manner at the right time is important.*
- *Sometimes it's better to remain silent.*
- *Balance in life, such as between home and work, enhances it.*

Oxyrhynchus Life: Old Woman Experiencing Invasion of Her Country and Culture

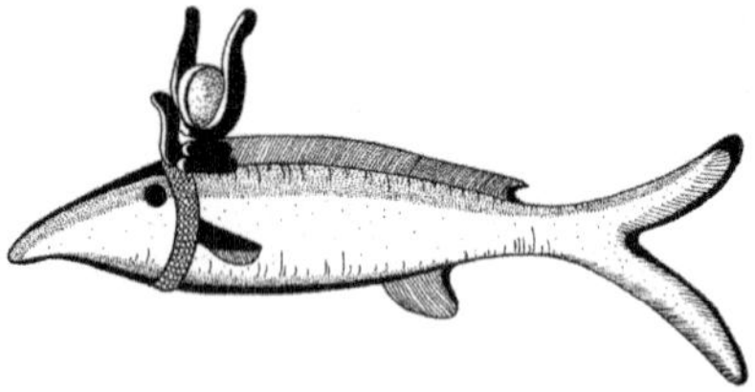

Oxyrhynchus is an ancient Egyptian town 50 miles west of the Nile. Oxyrhynchus means 'sharp nosed fish'. It was so named because a pike-like fish lived in the canal that had been dug from the Nile to the town to irrigate the land and to provide a navigation channel for ships.

I was a woman in my middle years, high powered and influential. I wore a cloak with a big stone on it, denoting my wealth. I was used to people listening to me when I spoke.

Octavian's army invaded Egypt, defeating Anthony and Cleopatra around 30 BCE. I have a strong memory of the invading army coming to our town and the 'tramp, tramp' of their marching feet. We were fearful of what was going to happen. Egypt became a Roman province under Octavian, who was quite a harsh ruler. We had to adopt Roman ways to survive. I was very angry about having to give up my gods and ways of living. I tried to influence the townspeople not to give in, but no-one would listen to me. I became very bitter and as an old woman lost my reason.

The experience in this lifetime started my need not to be controlled by someone else. Even now I struggle if someone tells me what to do. I can feel my back go straight and my shoulders rise. My whole body is rigid in resistance. I am all right if someone suggests something to assist me and without attachment to an outcome. But if I feel the slightest manipulation, I become very difficult. I have had to learn to discern the difference between kindness and control. This has caused issues between me and my husband, who for his own reasons needs to hold his loved ones close to himself.

Ironically, given my history with accepting change, I worked in business change and leading large programmes which brought much change to organisations. When you are changing peoples' work life alongside their fear of potential redundancy, sometimes emotions run high. There are challenges with calming people down and bringing some common sense and harmony to what we have been tasked to do. Always I felt it came back to understanding people and the drivers behind their reactions. As I noted earlier, you get much more out of me if you talk to me rather than tell me what to do. Most people are like me, in the sense of having an optimal way in which they work together with others and which you have to learn to understand.

I have had to learn to discern the difference between kindness and control.

In these challenging programmes, I always liked to have a good second standing beside me and protecting my back. Greg and I used to laugh and say that sometimes it felt as if we were foot soldiers in a battle trying to get change to happen in a business. We worked well together and we trusted and respected each other to do the right thing. As new job opportunities arose, we would follow each other into companies to take up our familiar roles.

Following your intuition and learning to discern correctly individual people's true behaviour patterns was key to our success. This is what Greg has to say on our working life together:

> *'I learnt much from Andrea about leading people. Andrea helped me to gain insight into understanding myself and others, which helped to inform how we could work more effectively together. This improved my overall happiness at work and ultimately at home too.'*
>
> – Greg, Richmond, Greater London

Change, whether it's at home or at work, is often a point of stress. But it's at that point in your life that there is an opportunity to do things differently so you can transform yourself and move forwards to a better place. In that better place with a better version of you, your expanded consciousness, with a greater connection to your intuition, can give and receive love more easily. Love is intelligent energy, so you have the opportunity to rediscover your own personal wisdom so you can use it in your everyday life.

Of course, each of these steps is significant – and you usually take small, incremental steps in each life you live. Each new life lesson you learn helps to expand your consciousness. Within your current life everyone is able to learn how to connect with their intuition.

Expanding my consciousness and relearning to connect with my intuition are things being learnt throughout all of my lives. I am often asked how I connect with my intuition. My answer is simple: it can be both quick and easy. You can even do it in the middle of a busy day when you need some guidance. I have done it in my office and even in the middle of a meeting. It can be wonderfully reassuring for your intuition to help you in your decisions.

Lessons

The lessons from this ancient life are:

- *Be receptive to change, assess what is right for you, and adopt the good elements.*
- *It is sometimes challenging to discern the difference between kindness and manipulation.*

How to Connect with Your Intuition

Take three deep breaths in through your nose and out through your mouth. Place your hand palm down on your heart area. Ask a simple question and feel in your heart if the answer is positive or negative. This is a simple yes or no and is your intuition responding to your question.

Peasant Life: Man Falsely Accused of Stealing Bread and Hung

I led a poor but honest life. At a time of food shortage, I was wrongly accused of stealing bread to feed my family. Without any real justice and no opportunity to give my version of events, I was hauled out of my home and taken away. The seniors of our community unilaterally decided I was guilty and I was taken away and hung. I was just a pawn in a power game where an example needed to be set for the community to see the consequences of stealing.

I was hung from the top of the town wall with the rope tied to a stake in the wall. I can remember being made to stand on top of the wall and the looped end of the rope passed over my head. My head was not covered with a cloth and I was made to look out over the crowd below. I shouted at the top of my voice that I didn't steal the bread. To stop me shouting the soldiers gave me a quick push. I had a momentary sensation of being in mid-air before gravity took hold of me and I fell, with the rope snapping my neck. My body was left hanging from the wall as a lesson to others.

Lessons learnt from this life:

- *Many of us will have experienced injustice at some time.*
- *Retaining a sense of your own values in the face of injustice is key.*

I feel it took some time for my soul to recover from this experience. I have died many times, but the injustice of this passing felt wrong to me. There is a longer break than normal before I am born again into a new life. I had thought perhaps there was another life I had not remembered. But when I remembered this life, I feel perhaps I needed that break before I was ready to live again in a new body. To this day I still struggle to wear a polo neck jumper that comes tightly up around my neck. Since learning about this life, that sensation has eased but has not fully gone away. However, I have a strong sense of justice. Perhaps it was born from the experience in this life.

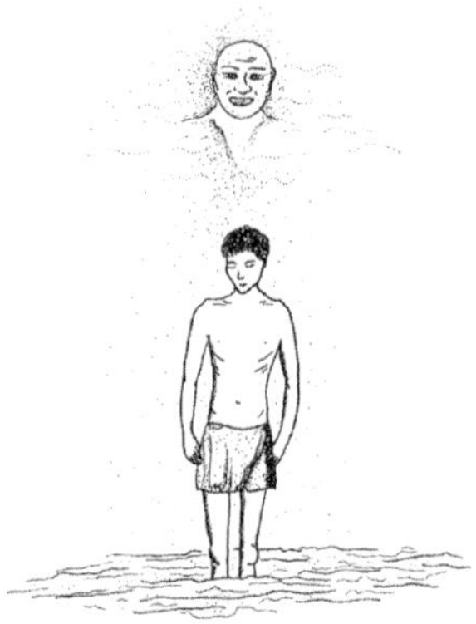

Baptism Life: Boy, Realising a Guide Has a Personality, Too

I learnt about this life when I was sitting in the bath and wondering why I could not remember any lives during the Roman era, given the length and importance of Roman culture to the Western world. Wang, my guide, is a Tibetan monk and has a great sense of Tibetan humour.

I looked down and saw a set of boy's knobbly knees and water with sunshine glinting on the surface. The water was being poured over them and the light sparkled off it. I was being baptised by full immersion in early Christian times. I sensed Wang's smile and laughter as he helped me to remember a relatively small aspect of a Roman life.

Lessons

Throughout my interactions with Wang, he has always remained positive about my attempts to develop both my capabilities and my outlook on life. He often uses humour to break my tension with myself. When I was struggling to find the right words for the third draft of my second book, Wang came and sat with me on my sofa with his feet up on a footstool. He said to me, '*Relax, the words will come to you. I will give you a helping hand.*'

Then I saw Wang had brought a chum with him. His friend was Chang, an ancient Chinese writer, who was leaning over my laptop and pouring energy into my book files. Wang's friend was doing all of the work! Perhaps this was a lesson in teamwork and asking for help.

- *Guides have their own personality and a sense of humour.*
- *All attempts at developing yourself are good.*
- *Never be afraid to ask for help.*
- *Difficult tasks are made easier when you work as a team.*

Roman Businessman: Man Sharing His Opportunities in Life

In this Roman life I worked hard to develop an international textile business. Once established it supported my family and my younger brother's family. My current-life daughter was my brother, and we worked together to develop and expand the business.

Recent archaeological work has identified that the Roman textile industry was much more sophisticated than originally thought. The Romans established factories throughout their empire, having learned effective loom building from the Egyptians. Dyes allowed the creation of riotous colours popular with the Roman people. Gradually, these techniques grew into mass production of a type not seen again until the High Middle Ages, a millennium later.

I came to remember this life from a stone I picked up in southeast France near the Spanish border. We visited a Roman villa that had produced wine on a significant scale and exported it around the Mediterranean. When I looked at the museum exhibits showing how the business was conducted, I knew that I had also conducted business in the Roman era and had really enjoyed it. It was the first time I gained a real sense of achievement by being highly organised and thereby gaining a better outcome. Looking at that life, I can see we had a highly optimised business process for the production of our textiles. This is what made the quality good at a reasonable price. We were able to replicate that process in many locations. This led to a successful business, providing us with a good profit and life.

It makes me smile to realise that the learning from this Roman life has been used again in my current life in designing IT systems to support business processes. It is another reminder that all we learn adds to our wisdom and can be used again and again.

Of significant relevance of this life to my current one was encouragement from my guide that I could build an international business to replace my employment and thereby be free to write. I had done it before and I could do it again. It was just a matter of desire and application.

Lessons

A key learning for me in remembering this life is:

- *Skills learnt in a previous life can be re-used in our current life.*

Impacts of My Ancient Lives on My Life, Family and Friends Today

Andrea: In remembering and reviewing these ancient lives from thousands of years ago, I appreciate that humans and their challenges, loves and lives are essentially the same as today.

Individually we evolve, learning our lessons the hard way through living a life and making mistakes, to go on and live again to try to express our lives in a better way. From this repeated pattern we gradually learn lessons, which transform into our personal wisdom. It's the difference between knowing that a way of behaving is wrong to trying that way and discovering for yourself that it is wrong. As our life experience develops we learn to live in a better way, to gradually become a better version of our former selves.

We gradually learn lessons, which transform into our personal wisdom.

We certainly get a lot of practice in living life, but what I think is so wonderful, despite some 7.8 billion people being alive, is that we manage to find and engage with our own soul group. Of course, we are born to some of them, but think about that chance meeting that introduced you to a person who is really important to you, such as a partner or a lifelong friend. These are the people who help us to live our lives to our fullest, alongside learning all we need to learn to further our own development. For me, the key lessons I have learnt in this period are:

- *Within each of us is a soul who guides, loves and nurtures us at all times.*
- *Keeping a promise to yourself is important to how you feel about yourself.*
- *If you don't succeed the first time, try and try again until you do.*

By the end of this phase in history, I feel these are the key themes to the lessons I have learnt and continue to use today:

- *My late father-in-law always spoke of* ***'the importance of family and helping one another'****. Taking the context more broadly to mean my soul family, which includes key friends, I really appreciate his sentiment and understand that life is better with your family in it.*

- ***Knowledge imparted with love is remembered with love.*** *This includes much of the life values and wisdom handed down through family generations. Listening to your family's wisdom and consciously accepting it or deciding to do things differently aids your own development.*
- ***Balance in life is key to a productive and well-lived life.*** *Being too focused on one thing is detrimental to your well-being and the well-being of those in your life.*

Lessons and traits I'm still learning:

- *Work life should be balanced with living a full life and spiritual development.*
- *Remembering skills we have already learnt, such as healing.*

Chapter 3: The Middle Ages: The Emergence of Religions Still Practised Today

There is no single dominant culture in this period, but significant religions develop. The Middle Ages saw the rise and fall of a number of religions. The Druids faded out, different types of Christianity, such as Celtic and the Cathars, migrated directly from the Middle East to northern Europe. Roman Catholic Christianity establishes itself in the West and seeks to dominate over Celtic Christianity. Roman Catholic Christianity's treatment of other forms of Christianity could be quite harsh, such as the eradication of the Cathars and, in more modern times, the Inquisition in Europe.

From 622 CE Islam is established in the east by Mohammed and then seeks to spread out from Mecca. Islam comes to Europe, primarily in Spain. Over time Roman Catholic kings challenged the Arab Muslims, with Granada and the Alhambra, the last Islamic foothold in Europe, falling in 1492.

The Middle Ages: Andrea's Lives

Andrea: After the Large Man life, I realised I needed to control my physical urges to lead a healthier, happier life. To help me with this, I chose to lead a number of ecclesiastical lives with celibacy, simple food and devotion. During this phase I seemed keen to try many different religions. It

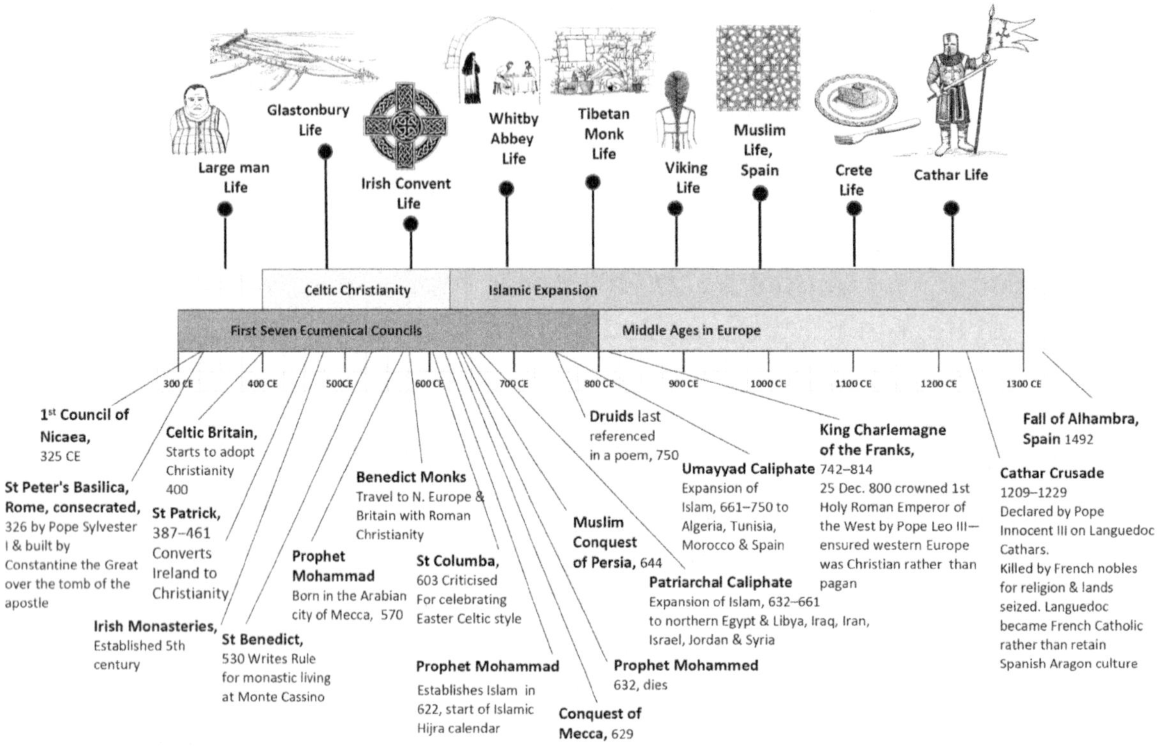

Figure 2: Medieval World Events and Andrea's Lives

was a turbulent time for religion in the West, and I sought to study and experience different aspects of them. I feel I was seeking to recognise while incarnate the reality of my life, the body I lived in and my place in the Universe. Each religion holds some element of the wider truth, but not all of it. I was sampling each to find its truth and to try to stitch the pieces together. I continued to do this into the Modern era. Perversely, in my later religious lives in the Modern era, I seemed to choose the religion which was not accepted in the time and place I was born, leading to some dire results.

After a series of ecclesiastical lives, I did try a life where I was married. Sadly, it ended in divorce, but at least I had tried. In the following two lives

I experienced the joys of a happy marriage. One of them was with the soul I had walked away from in the earlier divorce. Clearly, we were both learning better and kinder ways of being together. I find the developmental purpose of a life becomes clearer when you look at it as part of the story of your soul's development progression. You can see how failures in one life are picked up and worked on again in a later life.

Key themes in my lives during this period were:

- *New practises: divorce, Christianity in Britain and Europe, Buddhism in Tibet.*
- *Religions*: a variety of religions, including Celtic Christianity, Cathar Christianity, Islam and Buddhism.
- *Invasion*: I experienced the Romans Catholics invading the Languedoc and slaughtering the Cathars, of whom I was one. This reinforced my need not to be controlled.

The Middle Ages: Religions Fight for Dominance

In Rome, Christianity continues to develop but there is dissension within the church. In 325 CE the 1st Council of Nicaea is convened. It represents a number of different Christian churches with the purpose of resolving key differences across Christendom, including the date on which Easter will be observed. In 326 CE, the first St Peter's Basilica, in Rome, is consecrated by Pope Sylvester I, providing a key focal point for the Roman Catholic Church.

Celtic Britain starts to adopt Christianity in 400 CE direct from the Middle East rather than via Rome. St Patrick converts Ireland to Christianity, 387–461. Over 100 Irish Celtic Christianity monasteries are established in the 5th century. A dominant feature of these monasteries is a tall, thin tower.

Meanwhile, in 530 CE St Benedict writes his *Rule*, precepts governing monastic living, in Monte Cassino, Italy. Benedictine monks travel to northern Europe and Britain to convert Celtic Christianity to Roman

Catholic Christianity. Whitby Abbey is a Benedictine abbey established under Anglo-Saxon rule. By 603, St Columba is criticised for celebrating Easter according to the Celtic tradition rather than Roman Catholic rules.

King Charlemagne of the Franks, 742–814, was crowned by Pope Leo III on 25 December 800 as the first Holy Roman Emperor of the West. This ensured Western Europe was Christian rather than pagan. Finally, between 1209 and 1229 Pope Innocent III declared the Cathars in the Languedoc, in southern France, to be heretics and authorised a crusade against them. Cathar Christianity came direct from the Middle East, was more temperate, and challenged the corruption of Roman Christianity. This crusade was thus as much about power and land as religion. French nobles killed the Cathars for their religion and took their lands. This area then became French rather than retain their Spanish Aragonese culture, and the Cathar religion faded.

It is across this rich tapestry of change that Andrea lived her lives.

Large Man Life: Man with Overeating Problems

I was a large man through comfort eating. I did not love myself very much. I struggled with effective communication. I knew I did not communicate very well, which then caused problems in my life. I tried hard to improve my communication, but I found it exhausting and so continually lapsed in my efforts.

To console myself I used to eat. This then made me fat and ugly, so I despised myself and felt very unlovable. I really was not in control of my appetites.

Lessons

Even today I have an aversion to being fat myself and of fat people in general, as it feels like a character weakness to me. I have to be in control of my appetite, so I do not eat too much. Clearly, I remember the lessons from this life. Fortunately, my current body has a high metabolic rate, so I can eat hearty amounts without getting fat. Some of this is a result of my genetic inheritance. Even so, I grew up in a family of thin people and always felt I was the roundest so needed to manage my appetite. However, I am also a high-energy person, so I do wonder if my appetite is proportionate to my energy level. Memory of this unfortunate life has ensured that I monitor my food consumption with care.

The lessons I learnt from this life and still use today are:

- *Learn to love and be kind to yourself.*
- *All attempts to improve are good and should be encouraged.*
- *This reinforces the need to continually practise good communication to improve human interaction.*

Glastonbury Life: Man Using Shamanic Practices to Aid His Community

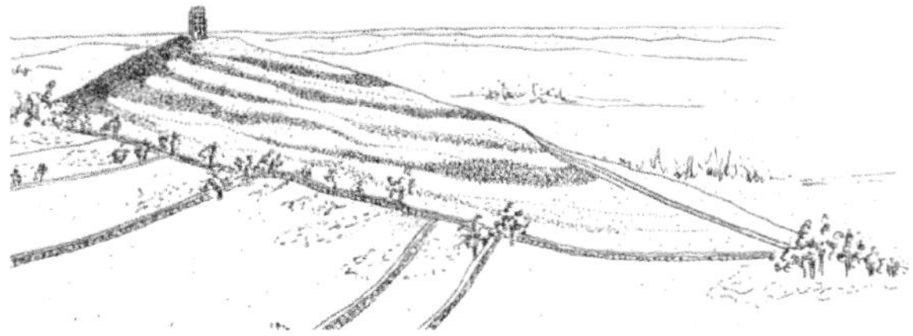

In the Glastonbury life I followed the old ways rather than the new Christianity which had become popular. I was born, as I am also today, into a family who remembered how to connect with Universal Energy naturally and without effort. This energy was used in everyday life to keep both family and animals well. I didn't believe Christianity could help me in this way, so I continued to practice the old ways. My family followed the sun and the seasons. I foresaw problems, as well as opportunities to help my community to thrive.

In my current life my Spirit guides asked me to seek out my shamanic roots, which brought me closer to this Glastonbury life and remembering how to hold energy in my hands to offer healing to others.

I was born into a family with a long history of farming in Somerset. I grew up with a strong connection to nature and the elementals in day-to-day life. Many of my family members are natural psychic mediums and healers, and we were often called upon when an animal was ill and the vet was unable to help. Through my growing years, my mother never suppressed any psychic experiences I had. She used to say it was good to have them and I should be thankful for what was being offered to me.

Lessons

- *Helping my community to thrive feels good.*
- *We can all connect to Spirit naturally; it is part of the capabilities of the human body and soul.*

Irish Convent Life: Young Woman Bored with Her Life

My current-life mother and stepmother-in-law were elder nuns when I joined a Celtic Christian nunnery in Ireland as a teenager.

A key feature of the nunnery was a tall, thin tower. When I was young, I used to look out of a window in the tower at the surrounding countryside and wish I was outside having some fun. The rules in the convent were very strict. I did not enjoy life as a nun and thought it boring compared to being in the wider world outside the convent walls. My mother in my current life used to say 'only boring people get bored', which used to make me feel unreasonably cross. Perhaps it was an echo from this former life and it was not the first time she had said it to me.

Although an elder nun and therefore much older than me, my stepmother-in-law became a great friend to me in the nunnery. I was very sad and lonely when she died. We had a special relationship in my current life, although I did not know of our nun life together before she passed.

In my current life, just before my mother passed my mother, stepmother-in-law and I had afternoon tea of a warm, sunny spring afternoon. In my heart I knew it was a significant event, but I didn't know why. The two older ladies sat while I made the tea, poured it and served it. Without realising it we were repeating the pattern of our Irish convent life. The older ladies spoke of their families, as they had previously done of the novice nuns. New members were noted, key developments were reviewed and hopes for the future were expressed. I listened quietly but didn't join in the dialogue. At the end of the tea, my mother expressed her thanks for a lovely afternoon and we left. The two ladies never met again in this lifetime. I have never discovered the purpose of the meeting, but I feel in some way the two ladies were acknowledging something from the Celtic convent life they had experienced together. By arranging the event and driving my mother to it, I feel I was keeping a promise I had made before I was born.

Lessons

- *Friendship is important.*
- *In loneliness and grief one can find an inner strength.*
- *We are never really alone.*
- *Promises made before birth are for keeping.*

Whitby Abbey: Nun Enjoying Companionship and Learning

When I visited Whitby during a course I was attending, I felt very comfortable there, and over the duration of the course memories of a life there began to return. I felt a colleague with whom I visited Whitby had been my friend when we were fellow nuns together at Whitby Abbey. On our visit to Whitby, I used to reflect or meditate in the vicinity of the abbey ruins. Every time I did this, my colleague also seemed to have the same desire. We kept our distance from one another and remained in respectful silence as we did when we were nuns together. It was only later that I found out she experienced the same surprise at our repeated meetings in the ruins and was also remembering a life there.

I was from an old family with wealth. I was at the abbey in the early days of its being established, when it was a place of education, more like a university than a convent. I seemed to have more freedom with my time than if I were married and running a household on an estate. Naturally, I undertook devotional service and reflection, but we had significant free time, which I made use of to study. I had a great curiosity even then, as I do now. The abbey was an open order, and the local aristocracy plus travelling aristocracy used to visit the abbey. As I helped to serve dinner, I used to avidly listen to their debates on social and economic matters as well as literature. I found it all very fascinating, even as I do today in my current life.

Lessons

- *Participating in a community is enriching to the soul.*
- *Learning is fun and broadens your perspective on life and the world around us.*

Tibetan Monk: Man Experiencing Sound to Connect to Universal Energy

This life came to me at a time I was exploring the use of sound to enhance connection with Spirit and to achieve more harmony in our bodies and emotions. I had learnt that the ancient Egyptians used sound in their healing practices. Using a method called 'toning', they manipulated the vowel sound using breath and voice to give therapeutic sounds.

Following this discovery, Alison and I attended one of Jill Purce's workshops on group overtone chanting, in which we learnt to produce a single note while amplifying vocal harmonics. The results were amazing – creating sounds like angelic bells. I used to follow along with her CDs on my drive to work through the countryside. As I neared work, I could see the energy aura around the trees as the chanting was heightening my consciousness.

This experience led me to the book *Living in a Mindful Universe,* co-authored by Eben Alexander, author of *Proof of Heaven*, and his partner, Karen Newell. Karen had mastered how to create sacred acoustics electronically.[12] They can be used in meditations to help you to enter and

12 **Sacred acoustics:** A technology for sound healing. It is a blend of binaural and monaural beats, and the frequencies are selected to provoke a shift of consciousness in the listener. Although it's challenging to 'prove' experiences of the mind, there are plenty of anecdotes on sacred acoustics taking people to fascinating realms.

engage with your inner landscape. By using sacred acoustics you can connect to guidance, develop your intuition, and gain inspiration and well-being. I have found it a powerful technique, and it resonated with a deep part of me.

When I met Eben briefly in London at one of his workshops, it felt like a synchronistic meeting.[13] Eben spoke of a planned meeting with Rupert Sheldrake, who is Jill Purce's husband. I recommended he introduced Karen to Jill so they could discuss their sacred acoustic work. I felt I had honoured a prebirth promise for this life.

Being interested in healing and the use of sound both to connect to Universal Energy and to heal, I asked the direct question of my guides: '*When have I used sound to help me connect and to assist in my spiritual development?*'

No sooner had I spoken the question to my inner landscape than I was given the experience of a moment as a Tibetan monk in a monastery in a subtropical highland climate. I was looking out on an inner courtyard which was open to the sky. The courtyard had a beautiful garden which I used to tend. There were ornamental trees, lush plants with big leaves like hands and an array of smaller plants of varying shades of green. Scattered across this green backdrop was a display of flowers in many different colours.

On this day it was raining. Large drops of water fell and splashed on many different surfaces – large thick leaves, small thin leaves, stone pavements, the barks of trees, the water in the fountain. Each drop made its own particular sound, but they blended together in harmony as if an orchestra were playing just for me.

---

13 **Synchronicity:** Synchronicities are not just coincidences meant to surprise and delight us. Spiritual synchronicities are strategically orchestrated and perfectly placed to deliver a message, provide guidance or provide reassurance that we're on the right path.

I lingered at the open window and listened. A joy, at Mother Earth playing a tune just for me, rose up within me. Instantly I connected to the Universal Energy as if I were in a deep meditation. It was as if I was connected to all around me – the stone of the building and each of the plants I attended to on a daily basis. I felt very rested and at peace in the company of my plant friends. It made me feel less foolish that I talked to them each day as I cared for them and watered them. It felt like they were singing to me in return.

Lessons

This simple, short memory reminded me:

- *Beautiful music can soothe and uplift at the same time.*
- *We are connected to, and influence, all that is around us.*
- *Love given unconditionally is returned unconditionally.*

Viking Life, Iceland: Woman Divorcée

I am the wife of my current husband; we lived in Iceland and were in our early middle years. We lie in bed together naked, but we are not getting on well and are arguing. My husband's hair is long, hanging to below his bottom.

My husband was good looking, but our relationship had challenges. Unusually for the era, Icelandic law allowed for divorce. I chose to divorce my husband and remember angrily cutting off my plaited hair, the symbol of our marriage.

However, after the divorce I was lonely. Past my first flush of youth and beauty, I found it hard to find another partner who was interested in me and I felt able to commit to.

Lessons

Once again, I needed to feel my own freedom and to be in control of my life. I didn't really try hard enough in this relationship to see if we could find a middle way so both of us could be happy.

- *Good communication is important for a good relationship.*
- *Working through a challenge is often more rewarding than walking away from it.*
- *Each of us is accountable for our own actions.*
- *Finding a middle way between two points of view is more rewarding than continuing to hold on to your own viewpoint.*

I feel that I took the lessons from this life really to heart. Finding right relations and a compromise both parties can honestly live with is something I have practised throughout my current life. I am often the facilitator in times of conflict at home and at work. It really resonated with me when I received feedback at work that I always sought to find the middle path for the good of all. It was if a bell sounded in my head: 'Lesson learnt!'

The Middle Ages: Islamic Expansion

The Prophet Muhammad, born in the Arabian city of Mecca in 570 CE, establishes Islam in 622, which becomes the start of the Hijri calendar. It continues to be used today by Muslims to determine the proper day to observe annual fasting and festivals. Muhammad conquers Mecca in 629 CE but dies in 632. The Patriarchal Caliphate is declared in 632. A caliphate is an Islamic government led by a caliph, the chief Muslim civil and religious leader. Until 661, we see the expansion of Islam into northern Egypt, Libya, Iran, Israel, Jordan and Syria.

Islam continues to expand under the Umayyad Caliphate. Between 661 and 750 CE, Islam expands into Algeria, Tunisia, Morocco and Spain. Christian rulers reconquered Spain, with Granada, the last Muslim stronghold, falling in 1492.

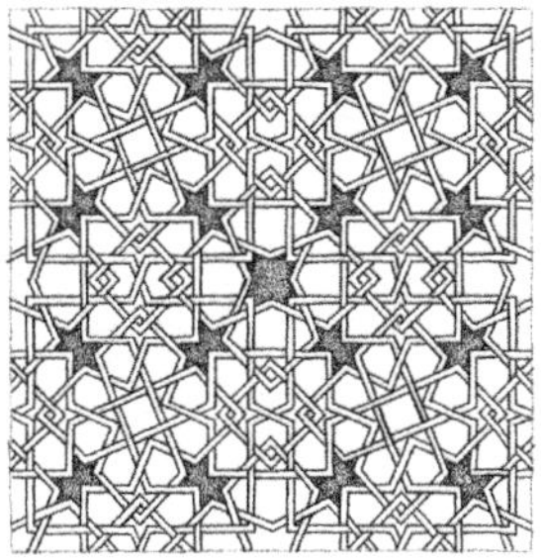

Muslim Life, Spain: Wife Protected and Loved

Both my husbands in my current life have taken me to see the Alhambra palace in Spain, which is a clear indication that it is important to me in jogging a memory. Each time I have loved the ambience, the use of water in the house, the gardens and the Islamic tile patterns.

In my current life I am particularly drawn to these Islamic patterns. With no figures or creatures depicted in the art, the colours and symmetry draw me within as I stare at them. I naturally and easily connect with Spirit. Calmness arrives and I feel my own inner peace.

I felt so comfortable in the Alhambra that I am sure I have lived an Islamic life, although I do not remember the details. While in the area I picked up a stone when walking with my current husband. It had a picture of him as a soldier during the battles between the Mulsims and the Christians in Spain. He was a soldier on the Muslim side, and perhaps I was his wife.

Lessons

I feel this is a key lesson as you explore your own inner landscape and past lives.

- *We do not always remember the full detail of a life but may remember cultures, places, trades, etc.*

Crete Life: Young Wife Deeply in Love with Her Husband

It took two prompts for me to remember this life. My current husband and I were on holiday in Crete and drove up into the mountains. We arrived in a village that is the last one before the road ends. It was an old-fashioned village, but the square was wide and spacious with a few cafes. Only men are sitting in them, chatting and drinking Greek coffee. It is cooler in the mountains and there is water in the streams and village fountains. We walked to the end of the village, which looked out over a lush valley of olive and fruit trees. I take a photo. I know it is significant, but I can't remember why.

We drive on and just before the road turned to head back to the coast, we stopped for a drink. The lady of the house brings us local mountain herb tea with a jug of honey to sweeten it. Unasked, she gives us some of her homemade walnut and honey cake. It is absolutely gorgeous, and I feel it is a gift to me to help my memory. Here is an extract from my diary:

'My name in this medieval life is Carissa and I lived in the village Andrea visited. The photos she took were where I lived with my husband and our children.

'Ours was an arranged marriage, but it was a good one. We had been good childhood friends and in marriage we found love. My name, Carissa, means grace or beloved. I am small, slim with an olive skin. My hair is black and shiny and goes down to below my bottom. My husband has a good job in our community. He is a little serious and perhaps a little gruff while he works, but when he is at home he is a loving and supportive husband. When I am working, I tie the sides of my hair at the back of my head to keep it out of the way. As I cook dinner, my husband's eyes follow me around the room. When dinner is over, he likes to unknot my hair so it cascades around me. He loved the time before children arrived as he had me all to himself. At night when we slip under our blanket to go to sleep, my husband likes us on our sides so he can curl around my small body and my long hair rests in his lap. He likes to run his hands through my hair and to wrap it around his hands. I can feel his love and it makes my heart ache. I have much love in my heart for him, too.'

Ours was an arranged marriage, but it was a good one.

Lessons

It seems to me that the nature of the times and the century make little difference to true felt love between two people. Carissa and her husband may have lived simply but they had found the treasure of shared love.

- *Love given and received is wonderful.*
- *A certain feeling of inner peace arrives when you give and receive love.*
- *Working in partnership enhances the experience and the outcomes achieved.*

Cathar Life, Languedoc, France: Young Mother Trying to Protect Her Child

This life I can remember in some detail, and my guide has taken a lot of effort to take me back to the village in which I lived this life. My current husband was my son and my maternal grandfather was my partner. We were part of a Cathar community in a village alongside the river Aude in the 1200s.

The Cathars opposed the Roman Catholic Church for its moral, spiritual and political corruption. The Roman Catholic Church responded by declaring the Cathars to be heretics and mobilised the Albigensian Crusade, 1209–1229, to wipe them out.

My partner was burnt alive at the stake in our little village square, along with the other men of the village. They attempted to protect the women and children who were hiding in a cave in the cliff on the other side of the river from the village. Sadly, the aggressors found us, and my son and I were bricked up in the cave where we were hiding and we suffocated. Outside the cave was a tree with a big black crow in it.

I have wondered why it was important for me to understand this medieval Cathar life from the 1200s. I have drawn the following conclusions on how it has impacted my current life:

- As my child in this Cathar life, my current-life husband understood that my religion and beliefs were different and that this was why we were hunted like animals and eventually killed. However, he had only a child's comprehension of unusual religions and the consequences frightened him. In this life he feels the echo of this fear and has an irrational dislike of spiritualism, as he sees it as weird and different.
- The Cathar life compounds my husband's experience of repeated lives in which he loses his loved ones. This causes him to want to hold his family close to him for fear of losing them again.
- My family home is in Crowthorne and its emblem, a crow in a tree, reminds my husband of our Cathar life. This is why he has an irrational dislike of Crowthorne.
- I have been claustrophobic in this life and struggled with using small lifts. This fear is probably explained by this French medieval life.

I am not sure of the rationale, but my guide Wang seemed keen for me to re-experience the actual village this life was lived in. As usual, my husband took us on holiday to areas of the world important for me, continuing to wake me up to the eternal being I am through the lives I have experienced. We had flown to Toulouse and picked up a car to drive south to the Languedoc. As we didn't know the area, I was using both satellite navigation (satnav) and a map to find our way. At one point I thought the satnav was being irrational in the route it directed us on, which wasn't unusual in the early days of satnavs. I suggested an alternate route. I got it wrong, and my husband was not very happy with me. The next day, he refused to follow my recommendation when I made another suggestion. Little did he know that my guide Wang had taken control of the satnav. Wang thought it was great fun. Here is how the morning went.

We were driving along beside the river Aude in a pretty valley with trees and grassy meadows when suddenly the satnav said, 'Turn left.'

I tried to persuade my husband that it was nonsensical to turn, but he wouldn't have it and insisted we followed the satnav. The road took us around a low hill standing on the right with a higher hill rising in front of us. As we went around the hill, we discovered that there was a village hiding behind it. As we came into the village, we saw a small square on the right with a school on the other side of it. A lane ran along the left-hand side of the square and beside the school, and then continued down to the river, where it looked as though there was a ford to the other side. On the other side of the river a slope ran up to a cliff which had some caves in it.

The scene felt strangely familiar, but I didn't know why. I decided to just go with it but remain alert.

Just beyond the square, the road forked. The satnav (alias Wang) told us to take the left-hand fork. The house inside the fork had some lovely flowers in the small space in front of it. But it was the house across the road on our left I was attracted to. I didn't know why but I felt it was a happy house. We dutifully took the left-hand fork and after a short time the road started to climb. We went up and up until the land levelled off. My husband paused the car so we could take in the marvellous view across the Aude valley to Andorra and the Pyrenees in the distance. There were multiple peaks, with each being their own particular shade of mauve. The vista was expansive, going from green in the near distance to hazy white with the mauve mountains rising in the distance.

It was a view full of serenity and beauty – and I had looked at it many times before. I remembered my life in this wonderful place. It was in the 1200s, and I was a Cathar woman and my husband was then my son. He was about five years old, bright and full of curiosity. I was a herbalist and gathered flowers and herbs to make remedies to help sick people. This was why I was attracted to the flowers in the village. I lived in a house opposite the flower house at the fork in the road. Of course, it wasn't the house that is there now but an older house in the same location. My partner was my maternal grandfather in this life. We have indeed partnered in several lives, although I never met him in this life. My mother often spoke about him as I was growing up, and I feel an unusually strong link to him.

It was a view full of serenity and beauty – and I had looked at it many times before.

In the Cathar life we were a happy little family, but sometimes I found the strains of being a wife, mother and working herbalist hard. I would walk up the hill to be alone and would sit on the grass and look at this wonderful view to gain some serenity. As soon as my son was strong enough to walk the distance, he liked to toddle along beside me to what became our special place. We went in companiable silence. As I sat on the grass, he would collect wildflowers for me and would put them in my lap. When it was the buttercup season, he would put them under my chin, so my neck shone yellow. In his sweet, innocent young way he said I was rich and lovely as butter.

Although my current-life husband is sensitive, he doesn't accept my view on life. But in that moment in the car in our special place from 800 years ago, he said that here was my view and the new house being built 30 metres up the road should be mine. I wondered if this was an echo of a memory from the 1200s or perhaps his soul speaking to me. Whatever it was, it was a lovely moment full of love and sharing.

As I looked again out across at the beauty of the mountains in the distance, I wasn't sure if I was seeing it with my eyes of today or those of the 13th century. Whichever it was, it struck me how steady and strong Mother Earth is. I could take in views of this scene 800 years apart, and essentially it had remained the same. It had the same capacity to inspire, to give me peace and joy, all within a few minutes. In today's fast-paced lifestyle, we seldom give ourselves the luxury of such moments. Yet 800 years ago, I intuitively knew the value of connecting with our beautiful planet and being in peace as one.

It struck me how steady and strong Mother Earth is.

My husband drove on. We followed the road as it went in a loop and brought us back down the hill to arrive on the other side of the original fork in the road. We paused there a moment. I looked at the location of my old home and briefly felt the happiness I had experienced there. I turned my head and looked across the small square, across the river and up at the cliff with the caves. This didn't feel good. My partner had been burnt at the stake in the square and the remains of my 13th-century body were somewhere in a cliff cave. The place looked peaceful now, but I wondered if the current residents felt any of the anguish from those times. New people had moved into our village and taken it as their own. Over the centuries new houses had been built where our homes had been. I didn't recognise the houses, but the layout of the village remained. Life had moved on, but I wondered if there was any local memory in today's people of the turbulent history of this now-sleepy village.

The car moved forward. My husband was totally unaware of what I was experiencing in my inner landscape, and I didn't have the courage to explain it to him for fear of breaking the magic of the moment. We came back to the main road we had left thirty minutes earlier. My husband commented on how strange that detour had been. Why had the satnav taken on us on this little tour? Little did he know how important those thirty minutes had been to me and how much it had affected my view of myself.

We continued on our journey in companiable silence.

In subsequent days and weeks, I tried to research the area and that village to see if there remained any knowledge of what had happened there. I spoke to a number of local people both on that trip and by email, but I could find no references to my 13th-century Cathar experience. I decided to let it go.

I am glad, though, that my guide had given me such a physical reminder of who I am and the wider horizon and memory that was available to me if I chose to acknowledge and allow myself to remember it.

Lessons

Humanity is often violent, leading individuals to experience harrowing lives with shocking events and difficult deaths. The soul carries those experiences on our behalf and tries to find the positive and the wisdom from them. However, such a passing as by being burnt to death is horrendous, and the soul can struggle with processing such a death, causing the experience to bubble up in subsequent lives.

- *Reactions and emotions in this life which may seem irrational can be rooted in experiences from previous lives.*

The Impact of My Middle Ages Lives on My Life, Family and Friends Today

Andrea: I came to realise you can connect naturally to Universal Energy or Spirit, whichever you chose to call it. Alternatively, you can do it by focusing your consciousness. Our human bodies are designed to do it, and each of us is born with the capability to do it. Increasingly, I observe people doing it easily and without effort when they are undertaking a creative activity. It is for this reason I find it sad that art and music are not valued subjects in schools today. Every child should experience this connection regardless of their capability. It has been sacrificed on the altar of academic attainment and the time formally dedicated to the arts is now given over to other, more scientific subjects. I feel this will change in the coming years as we appreciate more fully what creative activities offer us all.

Promises made before you are born to play a part in someone else's life are presented to you throughout your life. You do not need to seek them out. You may sense that something special has happened without understanding why. Being kind to others is your guide in these events.

Promises made before you are born to play a part in someone else's life are presented to you throughout your life.

Balance has started to arrive in my lives. Earlier problems of physical appetites have not risen up again. My intellect has been stretched and used to understand different religions and to connect to Universal Energy. With both body and mind comfortable, my emotions seem to be smoothed and an inner calmness has started to arrive. It is from that space of calmness I am now experiencing that I have come to appreciate it as a better place from which to manage my life. Better life choices are made from calmness, which leads to happiness bubbling up naturally.

Relationships with key individuals in your life may have started in an earlier life. You can reconnect in this life, nurture the relationship and/or complete unfinished matters. Experiences from previous lives can be your greatest teachers in this life with the added benefit of encouraging you to connect with your own soul for guidance and wisdom.

We all live in a web of relationships affecting all whom we touch, be it through conversations, acts of kindness or violence, love or hatred. You get to choose how you behave, but your choices affect those around you. Likewise, other people's choices affect your life but you are always in control of your life and how you choose to respond to a situation or a person.

Within my soul family, those I repeatedly reincarnate with, my greatest challengers are often my greatest teachers, helping me to strive to be the next better version of myself. Personally, I have found lost love and loneliness to be my greatest challengers. Finding my soul has given me great self-love and truly to feel I am never alone. I chat endlessly to my soul and always seek the wisdom we share, but sometimes I forget at a time of crisis.

Starting in this Middle Ages period, I have started to learn over time that love is expansive. It is not a matter of whether I love this person but not that one:

Can I love all of those who enter my life, including myself, no matter what mistakes they make?

It is easier to accept that love is expansive if you understand that we are all learning and trying to do our best.

I still experience personal love relationships, but I am finding my attitude to others is subtly changing over time. No-one sets out to be a bad person. Poor life choices may lead them there. But I am finding it easier to accept that love is expansive if you understand that we are all learning and trying to do our best. We are not born equal into life, and some people bring less or more wisdom into their life from hard-earned life experience. In the Middle Ages I had started to control my physical body but am still struggling with my mental world, so you see obsessions with learning and piety. Others may be further ahead in their development or further behind, but we all learn by interacting with one another. This is made more pleasant by being accepting of each other. However, this doesn't mean there will be no conflict or wars. Sometimes it is necessary to say no, your behaviour is not acceptable, even to the point of fighting for your beliefs. Resolution of conflict is about finding the middle path which brings the best qualities of each viewpoint together. This is not always easily achieved but is very worthwhile when it is.

Chapter 4: The Modern World: World Exploration and the Emergence of Science

This period sees Judaism and Christianity continue to challenge each other and the emergence of Protestantism. Alternate religions such as Theosophy and Spiritualism emerged in the 19th century. Europeans explore to the west and expand the world known to them with the discovery of North and South America. Sciences such as Alchemy, initiated by the Pharaohs, are adopted and made more mathematical by the Arabs. Science expands exponentially as humans examine and try to make sense of their world by observation and measurement.

Western cultures continue to develop, with art and music becoming more readily available. Territorial tensions in Europe lead to World Wars I and II. Terrorism on religious grounds has become a feature of the late 20th century and early 21st century. Economies fluctuate significantly and there is a crisis in the world banking system. The pandemic of 2020 brings global upheavals in health along with challenges from the lockdown of whole populations and economies. Russia invades Ukraine, and there are increasing tensions between countries in the East and West.

The Modern World: Andrea's Lives

Andrea: In this phase of history, I have additional recollections of my current husband's lives, even those I didn't participate in. I am not sure why

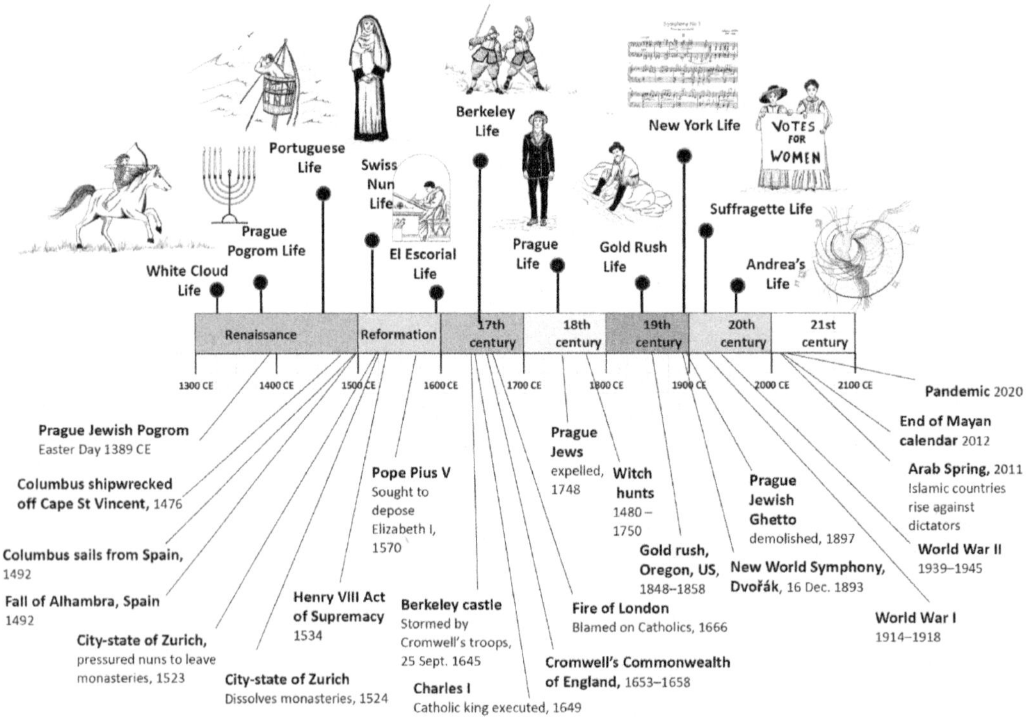

Figure 3: Modern World Events and Andrea's Lives

this is so, other than perhaps these lives are more recent and so perhaps they are fresher in my memory. I feel my husband and I are in the same study group in the After Life. I may know some of the details of his lives as we study what we could have done better. There is also the possibility that as we live together and things happen, I ask: Why is he like that? Please can you explain it to me?

In my current life, working on family karma feels like one of my objectives. It is for this reason there is such a strong link with the Greek Hellenistic life, which is the root cause of many of the issues. In some way I feel I am meant to use the skills I have learnt in the intervening years to aid resolution of our family karma. It is as if we have held over handling this karma until we were sufficiently wise to do it justice.

In this modern series of lives, I seem to experience a number of lives with difficult family situations but seek solace in a life in an ecclesiastical institution to regain my inner peace. During the family challenges, I am seeking to improve my interactions with others even in a crisis or very stressful situation. I struggle to manage my emotions of anger, outrage at the invasion of personal space, sadness at getting things wrong and acute shyness.

I need to use the skills I have learnt since the Greek Hellenistic life to aid the resolution of our family karma.

I have really learnt the value of kindness in these lives. I continue to strive to practice it in subsequent lives.

Latterly I experience the wonders of teamwork with my current-life late husband in the 19th-century Oregon gold rush. A life without a wife or husband seems a relief. I have a lifelong companion and enjoy the simplicity of working together. When you work well as a team and trust one another, the life outcomes are much better than when you work alone. Having had this balancing Oregon life, I went on to have a joyous life with my current husband with just the two of us and no distractions of children but full of fun and pleasure. I was then able to follow this up with a life championing the rights of women to vote and to be equal with men. Sadly, this life was cut short by the Spanish flu, but it enabled me to be ready to be born into this current life.

Key themes in my lives during this period were:

- *Invasion – as a Swiss nun married off when the nunneries were dissolved, and this was invasion of a different kind. Retaining my own sense of 'self' and my priorities when with controlling people was a necessity for my well-being.*
- *Religions* – Roman Catholic during the Reformation when Protestantism was the prevailing religion.
- *Speaking out for what I feel is right* – participated in the suffragette movement.

- *New technology/practises* – an early adopter of contact lenses, computers, mobiles and iPads. I became a female director in business, often being the only woman on the management team.

The Modern World: Jewish Religion and Spiritualism Challenged across Europe

Jews were challenged a number of times – for example, with a pogrom in Prague on Easter day in 1389, an event still remembered today. Prague Jews were expelled from the city in 1748. The Prague ghetto was finally demolished only in 1897. In World War II Jews were again marked out and sent to extermination camps in Eastern Europe. The Jewish population has never returned to its pre-war numbers. Similarly, spiritualists with unexplained gifts were marked out for extermination over the centuries. Witch-hunts continued to occur from 1480 to 1750.

In exploring westward to discover North and South America, Europeans found Indigenous people with shamanic beliefs who tried to live their lives in harmony with nature and the cosmos. Initially Europeans and European settlers condemned these beliefs, but they recently have come to respect them more.

White Cloud, Navajo Indian: Learning to Be in Harmony with the World

This was in a time before the Europeans arrived in America and life was more bountiful and carefree for the Navajo people. I was White Cloud, a strong, handsome young man who loved nothing more than riding his horse with his friends. They rode either bareback or with just a cloth between him and the horse.

White Cloud and his friends especially loved to race one another. The seniors in the tribe tolerated this behaviour, even though it was dangerous, as it taught the young men to be in harmony with their horse to try to win the race. Competitiveness between them drove them to try harder. The success of the tribe would be dependent on these men in the future being able to hunt together really well and provide meat for the community.

White Cloud was very competitive to the point of not fully listening to his horse and being in harmony with their joint needs. In a race with his friends, he pushed his horse too hard, causing her to stumble and unseating White Cloud. They both fell to the ground, sadly with the horse landing on top of White Cloud. It crushed my left hip, knee and foot. I did live but my body was twisted and never fully healed.

This changed the course of White Cloud's life. It was a hard way to learn the lesson of harmony both within himself and also with those around him.

Lessons

From this experience White Cloud learned to go within regularly to escape the pain of his body. When he recovered, White Cloud was a changed man and chose to follow the path of the tribe's shaman. He learnt to use the ways of the shaman to help to sense where food could be found and advised his friends on the best places to hunt. Even in challenging circumstances White Cloud found a way to contribute to his tribe's well-being.

I continue to have hip, knee and foot problems from my Neolithic farmer and Navajo Indian lives in my current life.

- *Remembering to sense within the right thing to do next usually gives a better outcome.*
- *Learning to be in harmony with those around you creates a better world.*

In my current life I fell and broke my left hip. The hip was pinned with a metal peg, but since then my knee and foot have always given me problems. I feel it was compounding my experience in the earlier Neolithic farmer life where my left hip was broken by a staff in a fight and also an echo of this Navajo Indian life. Whenever you have not fully learnt a lesson, you will be given reminders of a need to learn that lesson and demonstrate that you can live by it. The reminder in this life is to be particularly sensitive to those around me so I can help them to achieve the best life they can.

When my soul made himself fully aware to me in this life, he came first into my right side. I was very wary about the experience and was adamant that I should be in control of myself and wouldn't let him into the whole of me for fear of losing control. I remember thinking it was a shame he chose the right side to come to me because it was the left-hand side of me which had a weakness. Perhaps this was an incentive for me to fully accept the role of my soul in leading my life and to take him fully within it.

Jewish Pogrom Life: Current Husband as a Boy Experiencing Loss

My current husband experienced a pogrom as an eight-year-old boy in a previous life which resulted in him losing all his family.

I do not know why he survived while his family died but he is left to raise himself, living on the streets. He is clothed in a coat and boots which are far too big for him but do at least provide some protection from the elements.

This experience has left him fearful of losing his family but somehow expecting it. He tries to control his family, to keep them close and to prevent it from happening again.

Lessons

- *Experiences in one life can create anxieties in another.*

The Modern World: Expansion of the Known World

During the 15th century there were a number of voyages seeking lands west of Europe beyond the horizon. Columbus, an Italian explorer based in Portugal, sailed westward in 1492, 1493, 1498 and 1502, sponsored by the Catholic monarchy of Spain. He discovered the New World for Spain, landing in the Bahamas on 12 October 1492. With the defeat of the Spanish Armada in 1588, England began to replace Spain as the dominant world power, and Spanish influence in the New World declined. Britain's settlements were primarily located in North America.

The North American continent was populated by many nations from Europe in the 17th century, often by people seeking to practise their own religion without retribution. These colonies flourished and, following the

War of Independence or Revolutionary War, 1775–83, obtained independence from Britain.

The natural resources in North America were exploited. There were a number of gold rushes, including the most famous one in California in 1848 and one in Oregon in 1848–58. Music was composed to reflect the emergence of this new nation, including the *New World Symphony* by Dvořák, first played publicly on 16 December 1893 in New York.

Portuguese Life: Mother of an Adult Child Who Ignores Her Advice

In this Portuguese life my current-life brother was my husband, and my current-life son and son's ex-girlfriend were my children.

In recent years my brother bought a property in the area where we had lived in this Portuguese life, which was a catalyst to my remembering it. In our Portuguese life my son made the decision to join the New World voyages to America as an apprentice navigator. As his mother, I was really upset and angry at his decision. We could afford to feed him so I could not understand why he felt the need to leave us to go on a dangerous journey with a high probability of his never returning. I could not appreciate that the adventure and danger excited him. I could only see that he had not thought through the likely consequences. Neither I nor his sister, who was equally angry, could discourage him from going.

My son never returned to me, drowning at sea halfway to America. Even as I write this my heart aches.

My son never returned to me, drowning at sea halfway to America. Even as I write this my heart aches. The heartache was made worse by never knowing in that life what happened to him. It was a very hard lesson for me, allowing someone I dearly loved to make their own decisions. Both my children have retested my learning of this lesson in this life.

Lessons

- *You have to allow other people to make their own decisions about their lives.*
- *The hurt and anger at the pointless loss of my Portuguese son resurfaced in this life with great ferocity. It was only because I challenged why this anger was so strong that I learnt of this Portuguese life.*

- *Your questions are usually answered over time.*
- *Sometimes it is better to let someone you love go so they can choose to come back to you. They will do so with better grace than if you hold onto them tightly.*

In my current life my son told me he was experiencing feelings almost like drowning in deep water and couldn't account for them. I meditated on the situation for a while and came to understand that in this life my son is trying to practice good judgement. Every time he attempts to rush into something significant and does not consider it sufficiently before he makes a decision, his soul alerts him with the drowning feeling. In his adult life he is making key decisions on potential partners, his career and in business. The drowning sensation is a reminder from this Portuguese lifetime when he didn't practice good judgement and subsequently lost his life.

It was not an easy death.

Once my son had signed up to sail west, he was sent to the fort at Sagres in southwest Portugal to learn the rudiments of navigation. You can still see the fort today and the markings on the ground used to teach the young recruits. He returned home before he set sail from Lagos with his colleagues. I was too angry to wave him goodbye. His sister accompanied him to the quay one last time. All the way she implored him not to go, but his mind was set and nothing would change it. He stood on the deck as the ship left port. He gave a little wave and the silly grin he still has today when he knows his is defying you. His sister was so angry she threw her shawl to the ground and stamped on it. Even from a distance my son understood the sentiment.

The ship made good progress westward. The crew fell into the rhythm of the shipboard life and working together. The days slipped by. Unexpectedly a storm blew up and caught the ship with too much sail set. Huge waves crashed down on the ship causing it to sway from side to side. My son was sent up into the crow's nest to look for land. The captain was hoping they would be near enough to the Canary Islands to find shelter.

My son was calling to the captain, who was standing on the deck, and didn't see a huge wave coming. It hit the boat causing it to roll and my son was swept out of the crow's nest. He was young and strong and a good swimmer, so he was optimistic that the boat would be able to circle round and pick him up. But the water was deep and cold. It took considerable effort for him to keep his head above water. He bobbed along trying to ride the waves, but they often crashed down on his head and he was sent tumbling through the water. As he tired, his strength began to fade. He would catch glimpses of the ship, so he knew safety was not too far away. As time passed the ship did not come any closer to him and the glimpses of it were less frequent. He struggled and struggled to keep his head above water, but his limbs felt like lead. His head was longer under water and he was only able to gasp small amounts of air. Hope began to fade and he was faced with the reality of his situation. He looked down into the depths of the dark water and wondered what would become of his body. Would it be eaten by dark creatures of the depths? He had never liked dark places, so this death is not one he would have chosen for himself. Valiantly he struggled, such was his desire to live, but ultimately his strength gave out and he could kick no more. Gently his body sank into the depths. Unusually his soul stayed with his body right to the point of physical death, so he saw the receding light of the surface and felt the lack of air as he slipped into the icy depths.

Unusually, his soul stayed with his body right to the point of physical death.

In recent times, after I remembered this Portuguese life, the captain of the ship came to me. He said:

'Your son was a well-liked and respected member of the crew. Despite the risk to their own lives in the storm, we continued to circle the area in the hopes of finding your son. But it was a hopeless task trying to see a single dark head in a raging storm. In the end I had to call off the search and we had to sail on. I am so sorry. I knew his family would be so sad.

'We did make it safely to port and sailed further west. We didn't return to Lagos but went to another port in Europe, so I never got the chance to come and tell you what became of your son. I never found the courage to send you a message.

I have come to say sorry for not making the effort to contact you and leaving you not knowing what had happened.'

Five hundred years after his death, I cried for my son and the death he had experienced. I had not been able to keep him safe.

In my curent life, my son at the age of twenty wanted to go travelling to South America with a couple of his chums. This was before the times of WhatsApp and easy contact from most places in the world. Reluctantly, I had to say goodbye to him again. I had lost his dad to death, and I didn't want him to come to any harm on his trip. However, this time I did manage to send him off with a smile and a hug, not with anger. It was a hard lesson to learn, to allow those we love the freedom of choice over their own life.

> *'I was surprised Mum's gifts enabled her to identify the cause of my unusual sensations. At the time it felt relevant for what was happening in my life. In the intervening years I am not sure I have reflected sufficiently on the message I was obviously meant to receive. I hope as I have matured, I have learnt to think before I leap.*
>
> *'Thank you, Mum, for all of the love and support you have given me in my life(s).'*
>
> – James, London

The Modern World: Roman Catholicism Is Challenged in Europe and Britain

Roman Catholicism experienced some turbulent years in Europe. Due to a lack of suitable wives for its male citizens, the city of Zurich pressurised nuns to leave monasteries in 1523, finally dissolving the monasteries in 1524. The English king, Henry VIII, challenged the supremacy of the pope and broke away from the Roman Catholic Church with the Act of Supremacy in 1534 to marry Anne Boleyn. In retribution Pope Pius V sought to depose Henry's daughter, Queen Elizabeth I, in 1570.

Subsequently the Protestants under Oliver Cromwell challenged the Roman Catholic king of Britain, Charles I, and Britain dissolved into civil war. The royalists lost, resulting in King Charles being beheaded in 1649. During this war Cromwell's troops stormed the Catholic stronghold of Berkeley Castle. Cromwell established the Commonwealth of England in 1653, but following the death of Cromwell in 1658, we saw the restoration of the beheaded king's son as Charles II, but with more limited powers.

Swiss Nun Life, Zurich: Young Woman Experiencing Major Change

My current husband had a spell of working in Zurich. As I had given up my job, I took the opportunity to travel with him. While he was at work I used to walk all over Zurich, travelling on the trams to see the outlying areas and the boats on the lake. On one day I went to visit a museum near the railway station. It contained many old pieces of furniture dating from the 1500s. I immediately felt a strong connection to the furniture, in particular the large, highly coloured stoves which kept the rooms warm.

I started to remember a life as a nun but with my current-life husband as my husband, which did not make sense. Research pinpointed the nun's life to 1524, when the nunneries were dissolved and the nuns married off. Going from being a nun to a married woman must have been quite a shock. This was an invasion of my private space, body and lifestyle, which is why I had remembered it.

Lessons

- *This reinforced the lesson to be flexible in life and to embrace the challenges life throws at you; it can transform your experience.*

Spanish King's Library, El Escorial: Librarian Monk Absorbed in His Studies

In 2017 as soon as I entered El Escorial, the Royal Library, and saw the highly decorated books, I felt a jolt and remembered being there before. We were on a private tour organised by a Spanish company I worked for. Amazingly, we were allowed to touch the books, which caused me to move into another time. It was like I was watching a film and seeing myself in another time and life but at the same time experiencing the emotions of that life.

Before entering the monastery at El Escorial, I used to run free in the surrounding hills. I loved the feeling of freedom and the beauty of nature, especially the flowers. I didn't want to be a monk. It was what my family wanted rather than what I wanted. I wanted to live a life outdoors in nature.

A monk's life is cloistered and celibate. My freedom-loving soul was not comfortable with this. However, a monk I became and I found solace in the books in the library. I learnt to read and that opened up an inner world beyond the walls of the monastery. I admired the beauty of well-written prose conveying a concept across time to future generations. Colour adds energy and beauty to the written word. In the books I created, I added large gold initial capitals at the beginning of paragraphs and used my knowledge of flowers to embellish them.

I spent much time reading and studying in the library. It became my life. I believed knowledge could bring understanding and hopefully wisdom. I had a reverence for increasing my knowledge of all things spiritual and a gratitude for the opportunity to learn. Today, while listening to William Meader's lectures I can immerse myself in Esoteric Wisdom studies, and doing so reminds me of the pleasure I derived from the library at El Escorial. Such is the joy of study that I have to remind myself I have done a life of study before and don't need to do it again. I need not to be distracted and to focus on the energy project my soul is prompting me to accomplish.

As a royal librarian I had the knowledge of many spiritual concepts, but I had taken a vow of silence not to share them. I kept that vow, but

I poured my knowledge and heart into the books I created in the hope it would make the concepts more accessible to future generations.

Lessons

- *Knowledge is not wisdom, but it can lead you to wisdom.*
- *A constrained life does not necessarily mean it's a bad life. By being creative you can find joy in whatever is available to you.*
- *The definition of personal freedom is different for each of us. The freedom of your inner landscape is always available to you.*

Berkeley Life: Middle-Aged Man Failing to See the Impact of His Actions

Berkeley Castle in England was stormed by Cromwell's troops in 1645. I was Roman Catholic and so was opposed to the Reformation and Protestant religion of the time. My current-life late husband was my wife, and my current-life daughter, brother, and maternal grandparents my children.

I remember Berkeley as a town in Gloucestershire near the River Severn, under the control of Cromwell's men. One evening in this life I walked down the hill from my house, passing below the church which the Severn used to border. Then I walked up the hill on the other side and stood on a promontory overlooking Berkeley and where the inlet from the Severn used to be. It had long ago silted up and was now a dried-up dip but still did flood some winters.

I was still recovering from widowhood and used to take solitary walks in nature to soothe my emotions. My mind was relaxed and as the warm breeze from the Severn caressed my face and arms, I gently drifted into another time. I could see the glitter of the Severn at full tide in the distance with the inlet working its way across the land towards Berkeley. There were a few boats in the harbour and a bustle of people around them. The boats were from times past, with white sails. The town looked different, with smoke drifting up from each of the houses.

As soon as I thought, 'That is strange …' the scene disappeared, and I concluded that it must have been my imagination.

That evening as the sun was setting, I went to pull the curtains in the bay window at the front of the house, which stood directly on the pavement. As I looked up the street, I saw a small group of Cromwellian soldiers energetically marching towards me with weapons in their hands. I felt a stab of fear in my heart and stepped backwards so they couldn't see me. I thought I was being stupid and allowing my imagination to get away from me. I stepped forwards again and took another look. Sure enough, the soldiers were still there and almost at my house. I stepped back again and noticed I was trembling. The memory of my life in Berkeley came flooding back. It did account for why I had been so attracted to this house and determined to buy it.

In this Berkeley life I had arrogantly practised my Catholic religion openly. Under the Commonwealth that resulted in my being arrested and deported, never to see my family again. My wife was left to raise our family alone – not an easy thing to do, especially as a woman on her own in the 17th century.

My current-life husband was my chum in 17th-century Berkeley. His religion was the same as mine, but he followed it privately and carefully. As a result, he remained with his family and they flourished. Leaving my wife to raise a family alone created karma between my current-life late husband and me. In this life my husband left me by dying. I needed to experience what it felt like to have to raise our family as a woman alone.

Lessons

- *Tragic events are often the basis of a lesson to be learnt.*

Jewish Prague Life: Husband Struggling to Express His Love

My current husband took me to Prague for a winter break to experience the culture of this ancient city.

We went to a concert in an old church. It was much colder than the UK and we had not taken warm-enough clothes with us. To keep our hands warm, I threw my scarf over our joined hands. As I did this, I remembered a life where we were Jewish and married to each other. I was a tall, thin man and rather serious. My wife was younger than me, pretty and a bit of a flirt. I wanted to please her but struggled to understand how to do this.

Lessons

- *Sometimes it's difficult to show someone that you love them and want to please them.*

US Gold Rush Life: Young Man Appreciating the Value of Teamwork

In this American life my current-life late husband was my best friend and colleague. We were two chums who prospected for gold in the US.

My late husband was the practical one and used his intuition to find the gold. I was the less practical one, but I enjoyed looking at the glittery stones. Our partnership worked well as we had mutual trust. He found the gold; I was responsible for the financial side, getting the gold graded and sold. We had a good life together even though it was rough and tough.

Lessons

- *Trust is important between people who love each other.*
- *Working as a team we are stronger than working on our own.*

We are born into a family, but we get to choose our friends. I believe in the value of friendship. For me a good friend can be as important as family. It is about trust and love through the ups and downs of life. I feel I demonstrated it in this Gold Rush life and continue to demonstrate it in this life.

> *'Andrea and I have been friends for decades. We met in our late teens and together have been newlyweds, young mums, mums of challenging teenagers and young adults trying to find their place in the world. Now we are grandmas-in-waiting. We have coped with the ups and downs of life by feeling stronger by being together. Sometimes we have cried together but mostly we have laughed. I couldn't imagine life without each other.'*
>
> – Cathy, Bracknell, Berkshire

New York Life: Woman Living a Life of Fun and Joy

My current husband was my husband in this life as well. We had no children; life was about just the two of us being together.

We lived in *the* East Village and were possibly of Italian extraction. We were not rich, but we were not poor. In various lives my husband and I had been working hard on our soul lessons. This life was for pure pleasure and to remind us that life is designed to be joyful. We did not have children, as we planned to have a life just focused on each other and to enjoy ourselves. It is what I would call a 'playground life' and a break in our Soul schooling.

As now, my husband loved music and we loved nothing better than to travel uptown to the new Carnegie Hall to listen to concerts. He took me to hear the *New World Symphony* by Dvořák. It is a wonderful blend of Native American and African American music. It was great fun travelling there, and I was very excited before the performance as if I were a young girl even though I was an old lady by then. The first performance of the *New World Symphony* was on 16 December 1893.

When I think of the *New World Symphony*, I remember two periods in my current life. Most recent were the early years of marriage with my current husband. We were learning to live together with our respective stepchildren. By way of a break, he took me to Prague for time with just the two of us. Prague is a wonderful city with an outstanding blend of cultures and history ranging from opulent rich years to clashes between Jews and gentiles plus the austere communist years represented by their plain, square buildings. My husband took me to a performance of the *New World Symphony* in a beautiful old concert hall. Our pleasure of being just two was emphasised by our pleasure in the music. It was a much-needed reminder of the joy to be found in just living.

An earlier time was when I was in my teens studying hard for my GCSE exams. Stress aggravated my asthma and a common cold would put me into bed for a week to ensure it did not develop into pneumonia. In fact, I did my mock GCSEs in bed for this reason. My father used to drive to school each morning to collect the exam papers for the day and return the ones I had done the previous day. This was at my insistence, as I did not want to miss the practise ahead of the real exams in the summer. I knew my parents worried about me as I was the physically weaker of their children and they wondered if I would be able to cope with the rigours of adult life. In the early summer of that year I went into Woolworth, an inexpensive shop, to look at the make-up as teenagers do. Instead, I was drawn to the record stand and in particular a record of Dvořák's *New World Symphony*. I felt compelled to buy it. Fortunately, it was on special offer and I had just enough money to make the purchase. I struggled home on the bus with my heavy satchel full of books and my lovely new purchase, taking care not to break it.

What my parents did not know was that every time I played the music, I felt a great sense of peace and joy.

That evening I played it and in the following days continued to play it again and again. My parents were concerned that I was too serious. The teenage children of their friends blasted out rock and pop from their record players, plaguing their parents and disturbing their peace. From my record player came Dvořák's music. What my parents did not know was that every time I played it, I felt a great sense of peace and joy. I did not know why the music evoked such feelings, but I loved how it made me feel. There are worse things a teenage girl could be doing!

It is only in recent years have I asked why I have remembered this New York life and my love of Dvořák. My guide has said it is to remind me that life is for living and enjoying. The memory is for my pleasure.

Lessons

- *Life is for living and enjoying. Joy is good.*

Current Life: The First Members of My Soul Family Are Born

Starting in the 1880s, my whole soul family is born. I feel that this life is very linked to the ancient Greek Hellenistic life. That ancient life went wrong, and much family karma was created. In this current period, I can observe many relationships are working through the problems created in that earlier life. Some difficulties are thus being resolved, but sadly some are being repeated again. I guess we will need to come back and try again to resolve the residual difficulties to bring full balance into my soul family.

Lessons

- *We always have loved ones around us; we just might not recognise them.*

World War I Life: Current Husband as a Young Man with Failing Health

I learnt of this life when I asked my current husband why he was so attached to an old Tiffany lamp with a cracked shade, which he wanted to put in a prominent position in our sitting room when we set up home together. Naturally, at the time I disagreed with him but I have since changed my view.

My husband was a young man in the army during World War I. He was an ordinance man and responsible for a cart and horse supplying the front lines. He was gassed by the Germans through an unfortunate set of circumstances. My husband was dedicated to the job he did in providing supplies to the front line. He saw how hard life was there and wanted to play his part in making it as easy as possible for the fighting soldiers. He and his horse worked tirelessly hauling supplies to the front line and bringing back the ill, dying and dead. It wasn't an easy job. The return trip was often harrowing and the mud seemed endless, making progress slow.

One evening on a return trip with the dead, he was so tired he decided to stop and have a short nap to regain his strength to carry on. He got down from the driving seat and laid down under the cart, where he felt safer, to catch a few minutes of sleep. His mistake was not to put his gas mask on before he fell asleep. He was so tired he fell immediately into a deep sleep. In this state he did not wake up as the German gas drifted across the British lines and to the land behind. The gas moved silently, harming all life in its path, and my husband breathed in the gas. By the time it woke him up and he fumbled to get his gas mask on the damage was done. He was lucky not to be joining the men in his cart, but his lungs were irreparably damaged. Although he did not die, he came home from war with his lungs ruined and his health broken.

In the 'Roaring '20s' my husband lived in a single dingy room in London. Many exciting things were going on around him in London, but he was too ill to join in and this bitterly disappointed him. The only thing that brightened his room and his life was a single Tiffany lamp in his room. Aged twenty-seven, he died alone after a lot of cough, cough, coughing as his lungs failed. The last thing he looked at before he died was the colours in the Tiffany lamp.

It was a fast turnaround for my husband from one life to another – squeezing in one more life before we commenced important lives together to excise family karma from 2,500 years ago.

In this life my husband really wanted to live in London. Nobody could understand why. Once we had a small flat in London, we enjoyed all the great entertainments the city had to offer – concerts, theatre shows, art galleries, exhibitions, museums. In particular, he wanted to go to *War Horse*, a play about the role of horses in World War I. It resonated with him and he greatly enjoyed it. We have always said that we are like tourists, and of a weekend we go to an area of London and walk about to get to know it and enjoy all the wonderful architecture. London is made up of many different areas, each with its own personality. On foot is the only way to get to know it.

There were ten good years in the 1920s before the depression of the 1930s started. We are now approaching our tenth anniversary of living in London. It has taken me a long time to put down roots in London because at heart I am a country girl. My husband is now losing interest in London. He has done what he felt he missed previously and thinks it's time we went to live elsewhere.

My husband passed in the 1920s when the senior characters in my soul family were being born, starting with my father in 1920 followed by father-in-law 2, mother-in-law 2, and finally my mother. It would have been a fast turnaround for my husband from one life to another to be born in the 1950s. It is typical of his character to want to squeeze in one more quick life just before we were about to commence important lives together to exercise family karma from 2,500 years ago. Bright, lively and impatient to learn, he would not worry that his extra life might impact family members' preparation for an important family event. It makes me want to laugh when I realise that we take the essence of who we are with us from life to life.

Lessons

- *Behaviours in this life which are not understandable or explainable might relate back to a previous life.*
- *Whatever we miss or do not get right in this life, we will get a chance to try again in another life.*
- *We take with us into each life the essential character of our soul.*

Suffragette Life: Woman in London Learning to Appreciate Others' Lives

Having thought for years that my husband had squeezed in an extra life at the start of the 20th century, I found unexpectedly and with some amusement that I had done the same.

I was surprised when my grandmother came to visit me from the After Life. In life she had always preferred to be with the boys rather than me.

I was surprised when my grandmother came to visit me. In life she had always preferred to be with the boys rather than me. When I expressed my regret, she said she didn't know what to do with little girls as she had raised all boys. Once we got over this hurdle, my grandmother said she had known me in London when she was young. My uncle was born but my dad had not yet arrived. I was a suffragette working to get better rights for women, someone middle-ranking in the movement who wasn't known publicly.

As soon as my grandmother reminded me of my suffragette life, I saw myself working in a dingy little office. There wasn't much light. It was the middle of winter and there was little or no heating in the room. I was sitting at a desk diligently applying myself to paperwork. I assumed I was doing some administration or possibly writing papers for the organisation to distribute. I had a good brain and was well organised and articulate. I was well educated to function in business. I was a strong advocate of women having the same rights as men, and I tried to reach out to all types of women to help our cause.

My grandmother had an unusual background. Her mother was a doctor's daughter and well educated, but she ran off with a local greengrocer and my grandmother was born. This caused a rift in the family, with mother and daughter not speaking for many years. My great grandparents were not wealthy and my grandmother was not so well educated as her own mother. They lived in the East End of London, where accommodation was not expensive. As a child my grandmother had appendicitis, which drove her mother to seek her own father's help because of his medical knowledge. Unusually for those days my grandmother had her appendix removed.

While from a modest background, my grandmother informed me she had great sympathies for the suffragette movement, which was largely made up of women of means. Perhaps her mother had instilled an independent spirit in her daughter. However, my grandmother was a war widow from World War I, and my uncle was still a baby – she was a single mother trying to make her own way in the world. She said she had to be careful as there was no-one to help her if she got into difficulties. Your reputation was really important for being able to get work. She was sorry she could not have helped me more, and she had felt my disappointment keenly when she backed away from the movement.

Shortly afterwards my grandmother moved out of London with her baby to get away from the zeppelin bombing raids. She went to be a housekeeper for a widower and his three boys on the south coast of England. This man became my dad's father. And thus she raised a house of five boys.

In this Suffragette life I died in 1919 of the Spanish flu. In some ways it was rather a sad life. I was unmarried, didn't have much money to live on and had few friends. But I died working for a cause I believed in to build a better relationship between men and women and their respective rights.

Perhaps the slight awkwardness between us was not due to my being a girl but to the disappointment which sat between us.

Reflecting on the conversation with my grandmother, I have wondered if my suffragette life had influenced the relationship between us in my current life. Perhaps that slight awkwardness between us was not due to my being a girl but because of the disappointment which sat between us. In my childhood I didn't recognise my grandmother as someone I had known before. Perhaps on a deep intuitive level it was otherwise and influenced our behaviour towards one another.

I believe it's time to forgive and forget that disappointment. It doesn't serve either of us to continue to carry it. My grandmother was a woman of courage, and I respect that she came back to speak to me so I could understand her actions in a situation that led to my disappointment. I had perhaps been too high-handed in my reaction to her in 1918 and should have shown more understanding and compassion.

Lessons

- *Having the courage to say sorry is to be applauded.*
- *Forgiveness can lighten the load for all involved.*
- *Compassion is a hard skill to learn but can enhance your response to situations and people greatly.*

I find it interesting that I dived straight back into life with only thirty-eight years in the After Life. It's even more interesting that I chose to be the granddaughter of my friend. I know my own father is in my soul family. In my Soul Map he is in the bottom left-hand quadrant. Soul families overlap and live in soul communities. I feel my grandmother is in the same soul family as my father but doesn't overlap with my soul family as my father does. Soul community members often play a role in your life and you can reincarnate many times with one another. However, you don't seem to have the same closeness and intimacy as you do with your own soul family members.

Current Life: Andrea Learning to Remember Her Hard-Earned Wisdom

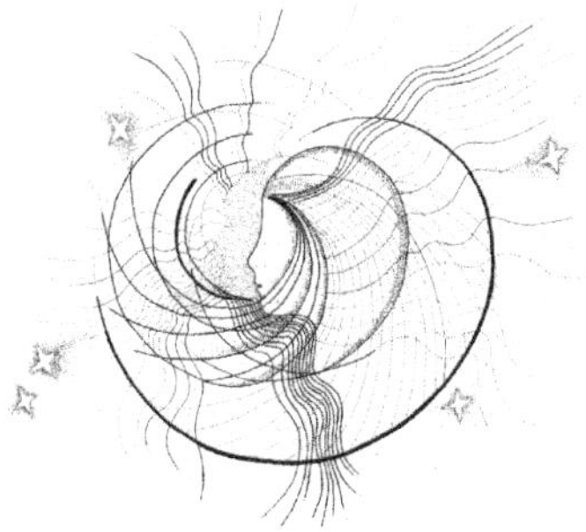

Born in the 1950s, I am a wife, mother, friend and colleague learning to share my experiences of life using communication skills learnt over 5,000 years along with the guidance of geometric art in Alison's Soul Map technique.

Born under the sign of Libra, I am developing a more balanced approach to life and pursuing a desire for right relations. In this life I have managed to balance raising a family with a demanding career. I have discovered there is real value in achieving this balance. As a busy working mum, I found raising a family was rewarding but physically challenging, whereas work was mentally challenging. Sometimes I looked forward to the days at work to rest my body. But when I went home my mind was happy to rest and let my body do many of the repetitive jobs needed to have a happy and clean family!

In the last twenty years I have learnt so much about myself, my life experiences and my own capabilities and wisdom. My greatest joy has been learning to communicate with my soul, feeling our shared love and remembering the project we came into this life to undertake. Following the guidance from my soul, the detail of the project is unfolding as I need to know it. Learning to connect with intelligent universal love has aided me to receive guidance from my colleagues and guides in the After Life. For me, this has been and continues to be an amazing journey not to be missed.

Lessons

My overriding lesson from all my lives is:

- *This time I awaken from a 5,000-year slumber to remember who I am.*

These are my lives, my experiences, my loves and lessons which I have been learning over the last 5,000 years. The process of remembering them in this life and recapturing my psychic abilities learnt across the millennia, which gave me the language of Spirit, has brought me great happiness. In this life I have come to know and experience that calm spot within and relearnt how to connect to universal love. Remembering my capabilities to hold and work with energy was an additional bonus which has added purpose to my life. In summary, what I have learnt is:

- *Life is for living* – the more you live life to the full, the greater the experiences you gain, and these are a catalyst for learning life lessons.
- *Love is expansive* – the more you love the more you are loved.
- *Life and love bring great joy* – living and loving, you experience moments of joy. Joy can be sustained. Life is meant to be enjoyed – allow this to be so in your own life.

Live, Love, Be Joyful

The Impact of My Modern Lives on My Life and My Friends and Family Today

Increasingly, the turnaround between lives seems to get shorter the nearer you get to modern times. It feels as if there is an increasing urgency to be able to lift your consciousness above the veil and to remember who you really are so you can be of greater use to humanity.

I am increasingly looking forwards rather than backwards to know myself and how I may become a better me.

I have noticed I am increasingly looking forwards rather than looking backwards to know myself and how I may become a better me. Undoubtably this has affected how I interact with my family and friends. My own children say I am very different to who I was just ten years ago when I worked in the corporate world. They say there is a greater kindness and compassion for others around me. Also, a number of friends have questioned me on my spiritual beliefs as they try to sort out their own.

I feel that my husband and I are at similar stages of development but have taken very different approaches in this life to move forwards. We both follow our intuition, but I have chosen to follow a very purposeful journey to understand myself, whereas my husband waits for his understanding to arrive when it's right for him to know it. That doesn't mean he doesn't think about his situation, but it's not overtly obvious to those around him.

Increasingly, people from many aspects of my life have chosen to give me feedback on how I have impacted their lives. When I have looked at the kind quotes people have freely given me, it makes me realise it really is time to wisely choose your life values. How you choose to live your life impacts many people around you, and you can choose for this to be a good impact. If we all chose just one good value, such as kindness or honesty, what an impact for the good it would bring. Listen to the feedback from the people in my life and decide for yourself.

It really is the time to wisely choose your life values.

Young people in my friends and family are increasingly approaching me for guidance as they try to find their place in the world and to understand more about themselves.

> *'When I had challenges in my life, especially during lockdown when I was more alone, Andrea listened to me and my aspirations for my life. It felt good to speak them out loud knowing she would not criticise me. Her listening and guidance helped me to decide what I wanted to do next with my life.'*
>
> – Tom, London

> *'Andrea and I learnt reiki together. We are in quite different stages of our lives, but we hit it off together from the first time we met. I'm a mum of lively young children. Andrea has done all of that and is now forging a second career in helping other people. Our shared values in life and our curiosity in spirit has brought us together. I love that we are so supportive of each other even though our opportunities to meet are limited. I feel this will be an enduring friendship and I'm glad.'*
>
> – Samantha, Dorking, Surrey

Older and long-established friends continue to use me as a sounding board for their life challenges. Often, it's about just listening so they feel heard and therefore empowered. Sometimes this help goes both ways between us.

> *'Andrea's outlook on life has made me re-evaluate what is important and meaningful. When challenges overwhelm me, I have been grateful that Andrea is prepared to listen to me. She is excellent at giving me perspective and focusing on the important elements of the challenge. With her support I find I have the strength and confidence to move forward with my life and be more contented and at ease with myself.'*
>
> – Debbie, Guildford, Surrey

In the early days of my being a psychic medium, sitters came to appreciate being more connected to spirit and to hear messages to help guide their lives. More recently, it has been more like a discussion and giving of guidance on how they might live their lives to the fullest.

> *'Thank you so much for being there for me. It means so much. You have taught me the value of not giving up on my life and working hard to making myself and my life better.'*
>
> – Michelle, London

The birth of new members into my family and friends with challenges, plus anxiety from the pandemic of 2020 and increasingly people with health and well-being challenges, have led me to practise energy healing along with healing from listening to someone's issues and providing kind, healing words.

> *'Through Andrea's classes and her kindly giving me healing sessions during my cancer treatment, we have become great friends. During our chats, Andrea has listened to the ups and downs and has always remained firm about a positive future for me. This has been encouraging*

and uplifting, especially on the challenging days. Andrea so generously gives her time, attention and gifts to help others.'

– Dee, Reading, Berkshire

As some of my family and friends more consciously pursue their own spiritual journey, increasingly they have turned to me to explain things that are happening to them, especially at times when their loved ones are passing or have passed.

'I have a great curiosity in Spirit. When things happen in my life, such as the passing of my mum, Andrea is there for me not only as a friend but also explaining things with patience and love. To help me cope with my mum's passing, I wanted to understand what she might be going through, both her actual passing and afterwards. Andrea took the time to explain it in terms I could understand. I found it very comforting.'

– Tara, Farnham, Surrey

Some of my spiritual colleagues have become my friends. We have shared our spiritual experiences to help us to understand what is happening to us in our lives. We have also had good challenging discussions on topics such as:

- Why are we here and what are we learning?
- Reincarnation – what do we believe and why?
- What about death and what is beyond it?

I have found these discussions in a safe environment invaluable in learning to openly speak of who I really am. I feel it is not without reason that this close set of spiritual friends includes people from many nations – France, Japan, Germany, those of Indian heritage and the UK. In this group I am not alone in finding value in our friendship. Two of them would like to speak on behalf of the group:

'In our group we talk about spiritual topics without any reserve, as we know everybody is going to understand what we are talking about and can relate to it. I am glad Andrea has started this group and it continues to thrive. Each of us in turn leads either a discussion or demonstrates a spiritual practice. I have found it stretches my thinking and I can experience different ways of connecting with Spirit. Thank you, Andrea.'

– Françoise, London, formerly of Brittany, France

'What I love about this group is that we can share our spiritual interests freely as an explorative and ongoing discussion. We have explored and continue to explore some interesting topics. I love that we are from different spiritual practices, countries and cultures, so the debate is stimulating and thought-provoking. I lead a busy professional life, but I try very hard to make our meetings.'

– Louise, London, formerly of the Loire, France

David is a special friend who has been supporting me in my endeavours from the early days after I gave up my job. We met in a class when we were both learning psychic mediumship. As I started to develop my own teaching skills and was holding workshops to help people to understand themselves, David kindly gave me the use of his home to run them in. Somehow when you are working for Spirit, doors open when you need them. David opened a few doors for me and in that process, we became friends.

'What I like about Andrea is that she never gives up. When she has challenges, she faces into them and tries to learn something from them. This includes quite everyday things such as a challenging builder who did work on her home and did not do all that he promised in his contract. She had the courage to call him out and to ask for honesty. When I had challenges in my own life, I am glad she did not give up on me either.'

– David, Runnymede, Surrey

Throughout my life I have made friends as I find my way along my journey. I often retain them for many years even when we don't get the opportunity to meet very often. Age and background seem irrelevant. What is important to me is the person inside the body.

My family and friends have given me many opportunities to relate to human life, which has helped me to remember and regain my capabilities. As I work more as a healer and psychic medium, it is as if I am in a classroom beyond formal lessons. My soul brings me sitters from all walks of life with every human situation you can think of. I need to learn and demonstrate I can handle them with kindness and compassion for the highest good. This has helped me to learn to work with my soul and to commence our life project. I thank all who have trusted me to help them along their life journey.

The age and background of my friends seem irrelevant. What is important to me is the person inside the body.

Everyone chooses their own approach to their life. But I would encourage you to let yours be a conscious choice rather than just allowing life to happen to you.

Enjoy your journey, remembering that the journey is as important as the destination.

And, as the French would say: *Bon voyage*.

Learnings from Reflecting on Andrea's Lives

Andrea's soul has used the story of her lives to reflect the wider reality of life and what you are trying to achieve by living a life. Your life lessons may be different, but the mechanism by which you learn them is the same. You do not have to remember your past lives to know what life lessons you have learnt or are learning. You are your best self now. You only need to reflect on your current life to know what you are good at and what you need to improve on. In your heart, when you are honest with yourself, you intuitively know what needs to be improved. The power of observation makes you consciously aware of what you need to do. It never ceases to amaze me when I do an exercise with someone on observing their life, how objective and kind their own observer is. It sometimes amazes them as well when they see what insight this exercise brings. In that same sense, as the observer of Andrea's lives, this is what we see:

Which Were the Pivotal Lives for Andrea's Learning?

The Spanish rural life as the Awakening to her soul and the beginning of her journey of knowing herself. The suffragette life where Andrea learnt the need for greater compassion, which she is trying to demonstrate in her current life. Andrea is trying to live by a higher set of life values she has consciously chosen. In between these two lives, there is much learning of individual life lessons which have steadily added to her wisdom.

Which lives stand out the most to Andrea? Rather than particular individual lives, it seems to be key lives which are linked:

Ancient Egypt Crystal Pyramid life and the current life: Andrea is remembering how to hold energy from Spirit and Mother Earth to aid healing and more comfortable living. She is slowly remembering the project her soul agreed to undertake before she was born.

Fat man life and ecclesiastical lives: These lives were about learning to control the urges of the physical body, mind and emotions to achieve greater balance. Obsessions became a problem in the fat man life and some of the ecclesiastical lives, where learning and/or connecting to Spirit became her whole life. In the Roman Temple life, she completely forgot to share her experiences of connecting with Spirit as she was enjoying it so much for herself. In the Cathar life Andrea was a herbalist and used her inner wisdom for healing. Andrea seems to remember more of the life when it is significant to her development and her soul wants to emphasise a learning. The Berkeley life was a re-check on Andrea's values, but she didn't get the balance correct, resulting in her partner having to raise their family alone. This has been re-balanced in today's life with experiencing widowhood. However, the Berkeley life did give her the gift of the experience of stepping outside of time in her current life. This was something new to Andrea. The New York life brought the understanding of the joy of living a balanced life which was done in relatively easy family circumstances. She now needs to demonstrate in a future life she can still hold that balance in more challenging circumstances.

Ancient Greek life in the Classical Period and the current life: The Greek life that went wrong created family karma which is still being worked through in today's life. So far much has been worked through but there is still more work to do.

Of course, all the other lives hold some value for Andrea's learning. She gains many life lessons by living, getting something wrong and learning to find a better way of living. All of these life lessons contribute to her personal wisdom, which her soul takes care of and carries from one life to another. It is this personal wisdom which makes Andrea unique as her set of learnings are unique to her. However, all of the individual life lessons are relevant to all of us.

Andrea gains many life lessons by living, getting something wrong and learning to find a better way of living.

Andrea has wondered for a long time why she has such a heartfelt relationship with her son. In this life he was a challenge to raise. From as soon as he could move, he always wanted to run away. Yet he has a big heart and a cheeky grin and always wanted to make Andrea laugh and be happy. But it was on his terms and not Andrea's. Her son's soul often appears in her lives, even right back to the earliest ones. In many of them, he is giving rise to a situation which tests whether Andrea has learnt a lesson. His natural humour is used to ease the tension of the situation. Andrea is inclined to be serious, so the use of humour in life is something Andrea is struggling to learn. Her son's soul is one of her teachers.

Andrea and Her Soul's Path of Spiritual Development

Andrea has been and continues to be on a journey of spiritual development. The life lessons learnt in each life are a mix of character qualities and behaviours. However, while doing an exercise to find how life lessons from individual lives supported particular life values, I found many of the life lessons were about an observation of the spiritual development process. I felt just listing Andrea's observations in the chronological order they happened in might help you to appreciate the phases of conscious evolution in a very personal and human way.

We will look at the character-building lessons later when considering life values.

For me, reading Andrea's observations one by one gives me a powerful description of what we are each experiencing, perhaps unknowingly. Here are the learnings about the path of evolution Andrea observed:

Many of Andrea's life lessons were about an observation of the spiritual development process.

- *There is purpose to being born and experiencing a life.*
- *We are never truly alone.*
- *In calmness we find our inner strength.*
- *We might believe we have learnt a lesson, but we often check in a later life if it is true.*
- *A lesson learnt transcends the lives we lead.*
- *Beautiful buildings can provide a space of peace and harmony.*
- *Outdoor space enables your energy to relax and extend more easily beyond your body.*
- *Learning to uplift another person is good.*
- *Love and promises are remembered across lives.*
- *Our actions in one life can influence a future life.*
- *We all make mistakes; it's part of the learning process.*
- *Our soul family loves and supports us through many lives.*
- *Soul families live in soul communities with community members often represented in our lives.*
- *Life should be balanced with both families and spiritual development.*

- *Remember to share my spiritual journey with others to encourage them to join me in the journey.*
- *I have successfully learnt how to connect to Spirit before.*
- *Be receptive to change, assess what is right for you and adopt the good elements.*
- *Many of us will have experienced injustice at some time.*
- *Retaining a sense of your own values in the face of injustice is key.*

- *Guides have a personality and sense of humour.*
- *All attempts at developing yourself are good.*
- *Never be afraid to ask for help.*
- *Difficult tasks are made easier when you work as a team.*
- *Skills learnt in a previous life can be re-used in your current life.*
- *Within each of us is a soul who guides, loves and nurtures us at all times.*
- *Keeping a promise to yourself is important to how you feel about yourself.*
- *If you don't succeed the first time, try and try again until you do.*
- *Learn to love and be kind to yourself.*
- *All attempts to improve are good and should be encouraged.*
- *We can all connect to Spirit naturally; it is part of the capabilities of the human body and soul.*
- *Friendship is important.*
- *In loneliness and grief one can find an inner strength.*
- *We are never really alone.*
- *Promises made before birth are for keeping.*
- *Learning is fun and broadens your perspective on life and the world around us.*
- *Beautiful music can soothe and uplift at the same time.*
- *We are connected and influence all that is around us.*
- *Finding a middle way between two points of view is more rewarding than continuing to hold on to your own viewpoint.*
- *Love given unconditionally is returned unconditionally.*
- *Working through a challenge is often more rewarding than walking away from it.*
- *Each of us are accountable for our own actions.*
- *We do not always remember the full detail of a life but may remember cultures, places, trades etc.*
- *Love given and received is wonderful.*
- *A certain feeling of inner peace arrives when you give and receive love.*
- *Working in partnership enhances the experience and the outcomes achieved.*

All along the way Andrea has been loved and nurtured by her soul and guides. She has never been alone.

- *Reactions and emotions in this life which may seem irrational, can be rooted in experiences from previous lives.*
- *Remembering to sense within the right thing to do next, usually gives a better outcome.*
- *Learning to be in harmony with those around you creates a better world.*
- *Experiences in one life can create anxieties in another.*
- *The hurt and anger at the pointless loss of my Portuguese son re-surfaced in this life with great ferocity.*
- *Your questions are usually answered over time.*
- *Reinforcing the lesson to be flexible in life and to embrace the challenges it throws at you; it can transform your experience.*
- *Knowledge is not wisdom, but it can lead you to it.*
- *The definition of personal freedom is different for each of us. The freedom of your inner landscape is always available to you.*
- *Tragic events are often the basis of a lesson to be learnt.*
- *Trust is important between people who love each other.*
- *When help is asked for, it can arrive in unexpected ways.*
- *Your own strength is available to you if you seek it.*
- *Working as a team we are stronger than one on our own.*
- *Life is for living and enjoying. Joy is good.*
- *We always have loved ones around us; we just might not recognise them.*
- *Behaviours in this life which are not understandable or explainable might relate back to a previous life.*
- *Whatever we miss or do not get right in this life, we will get a chance to try again in another life.*
- *We take with us into each life the essential character of our soul.*
- *Having the courage to say sorry is to be applauded.*
- *Forgiveness can lighten the load for all involved.*
- *Compassion is a hard skill to learn but can enhance your response to situations and people greatly.*
- *This time I awaken from a 5,000-year slumber to remember who I am.*

Andrea: I was amazed when Alison presented me with my journey to date showing the slow realisation of who I am so far. All along the way I have been loved and nurtured by my soul and my guides. I have never been alone, although sometimes I have felt that I was. I find just reading this list is so empowering and makes the journey feel much more attainable by anyone. Many of us are on this journey without even realising it. I see that key messages are mentioned more than once, such as *You are never really alone.* I feel understanding how it all works is very helpful and stops me from worrying that I am getting it all wrong. There is so much compassion in the help we receive. Just knowing we will not be abandoned makes me feel good.

Alison: The story of Andrea's lives and the life lessons she has learnt in the process are interesting. If we analysed these life lessons more deeply, we would certainly have a greater appreciation of the wisdom she has gained.

But what can doing so tell you more about Andrea – and, by association, yourself?

Before we delve into that, I want to talk about the marvellous physiology you have, which perhaps you may not be fully aware of. It enables you to learn from your life experiences and to retain that learning across your lives so you can compound your wisdom and slowly be able to lead better lives. Learning to access the wisdom held by your soul is exciting and worthwhile.

There are many parts to you such as the soul which make up the person you are. Whether you acknowledge them or not, they are still there working away for you.

There are many parts to you which make up the person you are. In traditional science perhaps some of these components, such as the soul, are not spoken of. Whether you decide to acknowledge them or not, they are still there working away for you. The design is complex and integrated and the science of it is amazing. You are born with all you need to have a wonderful experience of life.

Part 2

The Wider View of Spiritual Development

Chapter 5: Human Physiology

You have a body which is made up of a human mind, sometimes referred to as the lower mind, your emotions, and of course your physical body. You have this body for a single lifetime. At some time before birth, your soul joins your body.

Your soul is the part of you that lives over many lifetimes. For me, it is the true essence of you. It brings to your body a higher mind, sometimes referred to as your higher self, plus all the memories of your past lives. The soul brings memories of what went well, and not so well, in each life, in addition to memories of who you loved and the relationships you had.

You are born with all you need to have a wonderful experience of life.

From these experiences over time you gain wisdom. Your soul holds this wisdom as well. This wisdom, which is hard-earned from many life experiences, is what makes you unique. Only you have had your particular set of life experiences, so the wisdom you have gained is totally unique to you.

Your soul is almost eternal. It stays with you over many lifetimes until your wisdom has grown and you work so closely with your soul that you are one. You are then living in Christ-like love and you give up your soul to live as a spark of Spirit. In the esoteric widom, the spark of Spirit within each of us is known as the Monad. It has been present since you were first created millions of years ago, but only becomes consciously known to you as you draw nearer to enlightenment.

During your lifetime your soul will whisper wisdom to you – messages of guidance and love which uplift you. Many people seem to hear them the easiest in that calm quiet period as you wake up or go to sleep. For others, it's in the shower when the water is washing over you, cleaning you and invigorating you. If not at these times, everyone has a time when they are more receptive to their soul. At this time suddenly an inspirational thought will come to you to help you with an issue or a problem. This will be your soul talking to you.

From your first life your soul has been with you, but for many lifetimes it is unlikely you will have listened to the guidance from your soul. These lives will have been all about survival, and many of them will have been violent.

It reminds me of a child's toy, a wooden block with different-shaped holes in it. The child has to place wooden pieces of the right shape into each hole. Initially the child may try to put a block with the wrong shape into a hole, finds it doesn't work and get frustrated and angrily bangs the pieces on the block. Eventually the child has the thought or is guided to look at the shape of the block and compare it with the shape of the hole. The child will then learn to successfully place the right blocks in each hole.

At some point in a particular life, you will listen to your soul for the first time for guidance. It might be fleeting, but a higher thought will come to you. For Andrea, it was as a Neolithic farmer trudging along with cold wet feet behind a plough when she had the thought that 'there has to be more to life than being born, living a life and dying.' How right she was and her soul must have been so happy she had heard him. From that moment of first hearing your soul, which is called the Awakening, you will increasingly learn to listen more to your soul and its wisdom.

Andrea thought, 'There must be more to life than being born, living a life and dying.'

For me spiritual development is about increasingly learning to let your soul take the lead in your life and to follow its guidance. Even in one lifetime you can consciously take the decision to listen to that inner voice to learn more. Today there is much talk about being your 'better self'. This is really about increasingly listening to your soul and living your day-to-day life by higher life values to become a kinder, more loving you. You don't have to wait for another lifetime to correct mistakes you have made earlier in your life.

The Esoteric Wisdom describes this spiritual development of increasingly allowing your higher self, your soul, to take the lead in how you behave and live your life, in four key stages. Once you have experienced your awakening, you are considered to be 'on the path' of progressing through the four stages. The fact that you are interested enough to read this book would indicate that you are probably on the path.

You don't have to wait for another lifetime to correct mistakes you have made earlier in your life.

Before we go into the stages of spiritual development, I want to remind you of your intuition. This is another fantastic component of the human design. For me this is like an internal radio receiver and sender. It is a communications mechanism we all have which is available for you to use. Contrary to what we may have been taught, we are not designed to be alone but rather to be connected to other people.

Many people just use their intuition naturally and speak of 'their gut feeling'. I have seen senior executives in large corporations who need to make a decision listen to the facts of a situation and then turn and listen to their inner intuition to feel if the logic is right or if an alternate approach or decision would be better. Interestingly, they often place their hand on their heart area as they listen to their intuition.

Your intuition is, I believe, located in the heart area. Communication is usually by feelings and knowing rather than words. These messages are always positive and uplifting. If they are negative messages, they are probably from your ego and you should close down and stop listening to them.[14] The reason I wanted to speak of intuition is that the messages of help and guidance are not exclusively from your soul. You can be receiving messages from your soul, spirit guides, or passed loved ones. Initially you

---

14 **Close down:** The technique of closing down your energy and protecting it. This can take as simple a form as visualising yourself closing a door on your chest and locking it. Many different visualisations can be used to close down.

may not be able to differentiate between them and identify who is talking to you. This does not matter. If the messages are positive, insightful and uplifting, just accept them as that and make use of them if they help you in your life. I have to admit that for years I spoke to what I thought was a spirit guide, only to find out later, when discussing it with a colleague, that it was my own soul! We all have to live and learn.

First get yourself into that calm, quiet space inside and ask for a particular loved one to come and talk with you.

Some people particularly like to know who is talking to them, especially if it is a passed loved one. The guidance I would give is to first get yourself into that calm, quiet space inside and ask for a particular loved one to come and talk with you. You may feel a presence near you. Ask a very simple question, then wait and see if you feel an answer. For some people it seems to just arrive, while for others it can take some practice.

When Andrea's mum had a practical problem in the home, she used to get her late husband's toolbox out and ask him to tell her what to do. Together they then fixed the problem. Communications are not always high flown, but they are always given with love.

When I stepped out of corporate life to lead a more spiritual life helping others, my guide gave me three words: calmness – harmony – wisdom. At the time I did not appreciate the significance of the words and over the years asked many times if they were correct, only to get a resounding 'Yes'. I was encouraged to put these words below one of my Soul Maps which represented transformation. Trusting my guide, I use them together on my website. It is only more recently that I have come to understand the message they were conveying. It is one of transformation and the route which you can take to achieve your own development and transformation. It is perhaps why they called my visual representations of yourself and your life a 'Soul Map'. It is the route back to your soul so you may recognise your soul, hear its guidance and allow your soul to lead you in a better life. You do this by finding your calmness, creating harmony in your life and relationships and how you live your life. Through this process you will learn to access your own wisdom, which is held by your soul and has been learnt over many lifetimes.

Working with Your Soul to Develop and Transform

Step one: In helping yourself along the path of spiritual development to achieve your personal transformation, the first step is to learn to find your centre of inner calmness, usually around the heart area.

Meditation has become very popular, but being able to meditate is not the end goal. The objective is to find that place of inner calmness. Meditation is a great way to do this, but not everyone finds meditation easy. In my view, another way to find your calmness is to go for a walk in nature on your own. If you go with a friend, you will be chatting away or, if you are walking the dog, you will be distracted. Take just yourself out for a walk. Admire nature, look at the sky, watch a beautiful sunset or look at a lovely view. Don't think about all the things you need to do or the people you may be worrying about. Just enjoy the moment, and without trying your energy will relax. When you feel relaxed, take your consciousness to your heart and feel the calmness there. It is a very natural way to find calmness.

For the technical people among you, I feel that when you achieve calmness your heart and your mind are synchronised, making you much more aware.

Step two: From this place of calmness, you have the clarity to hear your guidance and to be able to ask questions of your spirit guide. You will need to keep the questions very simple in the early days of connecting to your guide, such as 'What is your name?'

In my experience, much of the guidance you receive is about looking at things from a different perspective, which helps to create more harmony in your life.

Step three: Harmony builds over time, and then at some point there will be sufficient harmony for you to hear your own wisdom, which is held by your soul. This wisdom has been hard-earned over many lifetimes, so it is well worth listening to and using.

Chapter 6: A Simple Model for the Steps of Spiritual Development

Andrea's description of her spiritual path is a very intimate one which might be hard to relate to your own progress. In a world so driven by measurement and achievement, I do get asked the question 'Am I an old soul?' The honest answer is that you have probably lived a life on Earth before and have returned again to live another life in order for your soul to progress.

Where you are in terms of your soul's development is somewhere between being a newborn and a very experienced soul. Through the stages of your development, you will learn to recognise your soul, accept its promptings, and ultimately accept the leadership of your soul. The fact you have a curiosity about your soul and are reading this book would suggest you have gained some life experience, but you will be able to judge your experience level better than me. No-one really knows the distribution of soul experience across the population, but if it is like other distribution curves, there will be some newbies, a peak in the middle range and a few experienced souls.

Many of the structures on Earth are a reflection of those in the After Life.

Many of the structures on Earth are a reflection of those in the After Life. The structure of your education and development as a soul is much like many education systems in a number of countries on Earth. There are usually four key blocks:

1. Primary / elementary / prep school
2. Junior / middle school
3. Senior / high school
4. University / advanced training

Then you go on to become a useful member of society in your chosen arena. These four stages of soul development are described in more detail later as part of the Esoteric Wisdom.

When I asked my guide if there is a simple model to help people appreciate where they were in terms of life experience, this is what they gave me. It reminds me of how an individual human's life matures over time from infancy to old age, but in this model you need to remember that this is about a soul's development. The wider definition of life is one where your soul lives for many thousands of years and moves from one life to another, taking their life experiences, lessons and wisdom with them. You don't experience this alone. The group of souls you started out with as a newbie progresses with you. You create strong loving relationships between you, and I like to think of them as your soul family. Members of your soul family will agree to play a role in each of your lives. Your soul family lives in a soul community, so it's a structured environment and not random. Members of your community may also make an appearance in your life, but your natural relationship is not as close as those with your soul family.

Each of these development stages reflects the prime driver of the soul. In each stage a description is given of the nature of the souls who have attained that stage. It doesn't describe how you get there.

1. **Understanding how life works on Earth**

   As you would when you start a new school or job or join a social group, your initial focus is one of understanding how things work. You want to fit in so you can feel comfortable and safe. This is important to your survival and you will follow carefully what others are doing. You will associate yourself with people and institutions you feel are strong and will take care of you. You will look up to strong leaders. You will also seek out members of your soul family so you don't feel so alone in an unfamiliar environment.

2. **Settling into living a life on Earth**
   You tend to live a quiet life, trusting others to know the right thing to do. You are happy to follow their directions and feel comfortable with the rules or guidance of your community and religion. You are learning the value of co-operation and teamwork plus the value of being part of a community. You don't want to stand out, since it feels good to belong to something. You tend to have a strong belief in your religion and can be uncomfortable with others' religions. Young souls are inexperienced and tend to be naive and look at life in a black and white manner with no shades of grey. They use the law to enforce morality.

3. **Pushing your personal boundaries**
   As you start to gain experience in living, your views start to shift on people who are not of the same family, religion or community as you. At one time you would have considered them foreign and not to be trusted, but now you start to see these people differently. A dad in another community loves and wants to protect his family as much as a dad in your community. You start to hear the promptings from your soul. You might receive inspirational thoughts on how to overcome life challenges in a positive way or urges to follow a particular path, which helps you to deliver your soul's objectives for this lifetime.

4. **Finding your place in your community**
   You start to gain a greater ability for introspection and to ask quite deep questions. You question how you are living your life and how you might make a greater contribution to your family and community. You tend to be the one forming societies and organisations for yourself and others. You connect more strongly with your soul and explore how you might lead your life in a kinder and more compassionate way. You have a desire for change.

5. **Desire to offer service to others and beginning to implement it**
   You become more concerned about the well-being of others and are keen to make a contribution to building a better world. As you become more aware that you will be returning to live another life, you have greater concerns about the environment and a desire to contribute to good causes. You have started to appreciate that we are all connected and you tend to be more flexible in your outlook on life. Your soul guides you in the contributions you can make given your soul's type plus the skills and capabilities which have been hard-earned over many lifetimes.

6. **Implementing a project your soul came to Earth to undertake for the betterment of humanity**
   You tend to be more peaceful. Experience has shown you that aggression and violence does not resolve issues. Personal freedom is of great importance to you. You are working more in partnership with your soul. You continue your own personal development, but you feel the urge to undertake project(s) guided by your soul for the betterment of humanity. You are sensitive, so the world can feel a harsh place. Full of compassion, you may avoid the news as it's distressing to you. But at the same time topics such as justice and equality are very important to you, and you may work very hard to ensure it happens. Likewise, teaching and assisting others to awaken to the wider reality of life and their soul can become your passion.

7. **Wisdom-based living and leadership**
   These souls are either living their last lives on Earth or are old, ascended souls who have chosen to return to help guide the uplifting of humanity. After many lives they have tried most religions, lived in many countries and cultures both as a man and as a woman, and in both poor and wealthy circumstances. Having learnt many life lessons, they are full of compassion and very accepting of others. Personal freedom and self-determination are very important to them. These souls hold great wisdom which they have acquired over their many

lifetimes. They live and breathe their wisdom and compassion, fully led by their soul. The projects for change they undertake will have a wide influence on humanity.

No matter where you are in your spiritual development, sometimes amazing things happen to you when you least expect them.

Andrea: I volunteered to be a trial sitter for a student, Barbara Ricca, on a healer's course at the College of Psychic Studies, London. I wanted to share it with you as it made such a difference to me to keep going with my spiritual practices, including my desire to collaborate with Alison for this book.

It was my fifth healing session with Barbara, and I had an amazing and totally unexpected experience.

I had met Barbara's spirit guide in a previous session when he placed his hand on my heart. He felt familiar and is a healer from ancient Egypt. I was reminded of my life in ancient Egypt when a wise man was trying to impart wisdom. I do not know the outcome of that lifetime, but it felt good to be working with Barbara's guide in this lifetime.

When Barbara and I entered the therapy room there was an unlit candle with a match beside it asking to be lit. I lit the candle and turned to Barbara saying:

'I have lit this candle to invite our guides to work with us tonight.'

Meditation to Open My Heart Chakra

Barbara led me in a meditation designed to open my heart chakra through feeling my emotions. In turn she asked me to think of a friend whom I love, someone who is neutral about me, and someone who dislikes me. In turn for each person, she then asked me to surround them in kindness and compassion. I could feel my emotions moving and was surprised by the different reactions I felt to each person.

Journey of Spiritual Awakening

Barbara asked me to think of the timeline of my spiritual awakening in this lifetime. She then asked me to identify three key events in this journey, starting from today and working backwards.

This has felt like a long journey for me. There have been a number of pivotal events, and I was struggling to choose the three key ones. My mind ran up and down the course of the journey looking at various events. I finally settle on the following, with the latest first:

1. Learning to fly outside of my body.
2. Experiencing my ancient Greek death again when I was murdered through a stabbing.
3. My husband's funeral, which was both the saddest and happiest day of my life.

Leaving My Body and Visiting the Cosmos

Barbara guided me in feeling the energy rising up through my heart chakra to my third eye and on to my crown chakra. It was rich and strong and rose in a column up above my head and out of the building. She asked me to follow the energy up out of the building and to look down on London. There I met her guide above me with my own guide reassuringly standing to the right and slightly behind me. He was sending me love and encouragement. I went with Barbara's guide higher, up above the UK and then the world. I looked back down at Mother Earth and all of her beauty, a wonderful blue and loving planet.

I then turned my attention to our universe with each of its planets, then further up to the galaxy which had lots of different colours swirling around it. Finally, we went out to the Cosmos beyond anything that humans know of or could explain. It is a place of love, light and angelic music.

I was invited to ask a question.

After a moment's thought I asked:

> *'My life purpose is to be a messenger to help kick-start individuals on their own spiritual awakening. How do I find the inspiration and ideas for messages to convey which people will be interested in listening to?'*

I was given a picture of a big funnel which ran from Earth to where we were. I was told that this was the funnel in which people travelled from Earth when they died to get home to the After Life. It was also where people placed their worries while in their physical lives so they could be heard.

When I needed inspiration all I had to do was stand in the funnel and listen to people's worries. Then I should convey messages which help people to overcome their problems. I needed to help them to go beyond their pain. These messages needed to be conveyed in everyday language with 21st-century examples. I have been allowed to remember a few of my past lives, as they are rich with human examples of love, loss and tragedy. I need to tell the stories of my life events but place them in a 21st-century setting so people can understand them and not feel pressured to believe in past lives.

When you relay the event, try to evoke people's emotions. This will make people connect with the message. The more an individual consciously experiences emotions, the more they connect with the Universal Energy. This will help to kick-start their Awakening.

Re-experiencing My Husband's Funeral

This was one of the early events in my awakening in this life and the last one I chose in my meditation with Barbara. My husband's funeral was both the saddest and happiest moment in my life.

We were singing the first hymn over my husband's coffin, when I asked myself:

> *'How could this be? A few days ago, we were living a normal, happy life with loads of plans on what we wanted to do together. Now I was burying him. Surely this cannot be the end?'*

As soon as I had this thought my husband was standing in front of me in full evening dress with a cheeky grin. He put out his hand for me to join him in a dance. As my soul stepped out of my body to join him, I was dressed in a beautiful three-quarter-length red evening dress, tight at the waist with petticoats holding out the dress. I moved into his arms and we danced round and round going higher and higher. I was having such fun, the movement, the swirling faster and faster, and feeling my husband's love. My long hair flew outwards, my lungs filled with air and I laughed. It was so different from how I was a few moments ago. As soon as I had the thought:

'This is wonderful – but how can it be? You are dead!'

The moment was gone and I was whisked back into my body and the finishing of the hymn.

As I relived this moment with the Egyptian guide, my heart ached so hard and a tear ran down my cheek. See, said the Egyptian guide, emotions open the heart chakra. You can feel it now. This opening allows kindness and compassion to flourish. Your stories and messages need to evoke a similar intensity in others. It is a message they will not forget as they associate it with an event with a loved one.

We all have the physiology to experience these altered states of consciousness, we have just forgotten how to do it.

I am reminded of the book by Gregg Braden I am reading at the moment – *Human by Design*. In this book Gregg says that we all have the physiology to experience these altered states of consciousness, we have just forgotten how to do it. At moments of stress, like my husband's funeral, we can naturally slip into it.

I have never spoken to anyone about this experience, as I thought that perhaps I was a little demented with grief. However, since then I have found out that this type of event is not unusual with the death of a loved one. Our loved one has entered the funnel, but if we join with them, even for a few moments, we can experience an altered conscious state and communicate with one another. When I accepted my husband's invitation to dance, this is just what I did.

Integration of Past Life Events and Their Life Lessons

My task is to get people to remember their key life moments and to integrate them into a life model based on their Soul Map. They need to feel the emotion and then to reflect on their life lesson from that event.

'What do you think the life lesson was for you in the death of your husband?'

The answer is simple:

'While he was alive, I did not appreciate the strength of his love for me and the freedom and personal strength he gave me unconditionally. I have only come to understand that as his widow.'

Well, that was not so hard for you to articulate. Your husband was a generous man. His death was key to your development. You need to find a model and process that leads people through the same thought process. It is about getting them to understand 'who they are' and perhaps change their behaviour to be 'who they want to be'.

With that the Egyptian guide placed his hand on my heart for a second time. This time there was an enormous burst of energy which radiated out from my heart to every part of my body. My whole body was left tingling.

After the Healing

Barbara and I shared our experiences. Barbara had received the same messages but in symbols that were relevant to her.

Barbara is Italian and had studied for her degree in Venice. In Venice, the Lion of St Mark is famous for his book of messages. The lion represents Mark the Evangelist and is depicted in the form of a winged lion holding a Bible. The lion is the symbol of the city of Venice and formerly of the Venetian Republic.

Barbara understood that this healing was about receiving messages.

Barbara's guide was an Egyptian, which she felt was significant to the message Andrea was receiving. There is a link between Venice and Egypt.

Venetian tradition states that when Mark was travelling through Europe, he arrived at a lagoon in Venice. There an angel appeared to him and said, 'Peace be with thee, O Mark, my evangelist. Here thy body will rest.' Mark returned to Alexandria in Egypt, where he founded the first Christian church.

Barbara and I thanked our guides for working with us.

St Mark has been considered as Venice's patron saint from the time his remains were stolen from a tomb in Alexandria by two merchants and brought to Venice in 828 CE. The angel's prediction indeed came about.

Barbara also experienced my 'dance of our souls' at my husband's funeral. She saw the Grim Reaper and his scythe, representing death, and she saw our dance as a great burst of light and energy soaring upwards.

Before we left, Barbara and I thanked our guides for working with us and blew out the candle.

Chapter 7: Esoteric Wisdom and the Stages of Spiritual Development

Many people inadvertently overestimate their life experience, lessons learnt and wisdom gained. To a certain extent it is irrelevant where you are on the experience steps. What is much more important is that you have a desire to progress and to live a better life with the gift of the life you have now.

The simple model presented in the previous chapter may be enough for you. In that case, you can skip to the next chapter. However, if you would like to examine this framework in greater detail and depth, this chapter provides an overview of the Esoteric Wisdom's stages of development.[15] Wider reading in this wisdom will give you more guidance on how you might develop.

If you choose to look at yourself against these criteria, please do so with caution. My teacher tells me that most people overestimate the stage of development they have reached. Most of us are in the earlier stages. Even if we feel we have had a kundalini experience,[16] it may actually be

---

15 **Esoteric definition:** Esoteric means 'not known by, or suitable for, most people', 'not taught publically', or, in general, 'rare or hidden knowledge'. Esoteric knowledge and practices include, for example, advanced science, mysticism, and magic. Intended for or likely to be understood by only a small number of people with a specialised knowledge or interest.

16 **Kundalini:** A kundalini Awakening is a form of energetic awakening that causes us to transform on the mental, emotional and spiritual levels.

an earlier stage and a preparation, with only one or two chakras passing energy.

Once the Awakening has occurred, you work on gaining mastery of your physical body, emotions and mind. Writing it down in this order implies that this work is sequential. In the physical world, we mark progression in terms of time. However, your soul takes a more holistic view on progress and can be working on physical mastery at the same time as emotional mastery. It is therefore more about quality rather than quantity of focus. Even when you have achieved physical mastery, the soul can choose to recheck your capability in a later life. All of this means that defining where you may be in your development is not a simple check like stepping on a scale or measuring your height.

Most of human existence is before the Awakening, when you first recognise there is an eternal element of yourself.

Most of human existence is before the Awakening, when you first recognise there is an eternal element of yourself as well as your personality (ego). You may have lived hundreds or even thousands of lives prior to the Awakening. Once the Awakening has happened, there is a desire to become more like the eternal part of yourself and to transform your lower nature to be more aligned to your soul. The rate at which you pass through the Initiations of consciousness development will depend on your intent to progress. Development takes effort and is deliberate. You may choose to let it happen naturally and more slowly, or you may choose to be focused and proceed at an accelerated pace. However, even with intent, numerous lives are spent working on each stage of development. There are three key stages of development, called Initiations, with the fourth stage being Enlightenment. Each Initiation is a measure of how much the soul is leading the personality. While there is undoubtedly a sense of progression from one Initiation to another, you may well be working on the qualities of more than one initiation at the same time, for example, your emotions at the same time as your physical appetites.

The *First Initiation* is about mastery over physical appetites and demonstrating increasing heart qualities of love and compassion.

At the *Second Initiation* you demonstrate mastery over your emotions without repression. This is a difficult Initiation, where you need to be more tempered and effective with your emotions and not to be led by them.

The *Third Initiation* is about demonstrating mastery over the mind and the entire personality.

Let's go into each of these in a little more detail.

The Awakening

Every human is made up of three parts – the lower mind, emotions and the physical body, sometimes known as the personality or ego. Initial human development is about getting these three parts of the personality integrated and working together. Although the personality is worldly and self-serving in its views, it is still a powerful entity. Many of the most successful people in the world today are at this stage. Some people live a number of lives at this stage before they recognise even a flicker of the soul and give it some listening. Only when the personality is ready for the soul will the soul start to integrate with the personality. In one life the personality will start to recognise the soul and the evolution of human consciousness can begin. To such a person, it is an awakening to a spiritual dimension within himself. It is an encounter with Christ-like love combined with a sense of joy. This is the beginning of what is known in occult terms as the Probationary Path.

The Awakening: the personality starts to recognise the soul and the evolution of human consciousness can begin.

A probationer commits to bringing their personality under control and to build character and behavioural qualities that are missing. The person tries to be a useful member of society and is often focused on spiritual practises which assist the physical body and enhance its well-being. This might include improving one's diet and including sufficient exercise in daily life. This period in evolution can take a number of lives, so it is easy to become obsessed with these physical disciplines. Initially the probationer may wish to create a physical body worthy of the lord. Over time this moves to the whole personality – mind, emotion and body as a suitable place for the lord. Sometimes they mistake the soul as being the lord.

The desire to purify the body is a common characteristic of the Probationary Path. Over time this will also include their thoughts and emotions as well. In esoteric terms, the perceived duality between God and human comes from the limitations of the human mind. Oneness between the individual and Universal Energy is present as it always has been, but the human mind is unable to appreciate it. In seeking their soul's purpose some probationers jump from one spiritual practise to another until they realise slow development is more enduring and all they must do is turn up and try to be the best person they can.

First Initiation

The First Intiation: the soul has mastered the cravings of the flesh and controls the body.

Increasingly the soul is able to express its love and wisdom through the personality in service to humanity. However, the personality has a role to play in this process by adding human warmth and a grounded nature to the soul's ideas, making them more receptive to other humans.

The soul's ability to influence and lead the human's three elements commences with the physical body first, then the emotions and finally the mind. This is a key principle of the Initiation stages.

At the First Initiation, you take your initial step in coming closer to your soul. At subsequent initiations you move closer. When fully integrated with your soul, your soul will be able to demonstrate that it can fully express itself through the human body, emotions and mind. Needless to say, this takes many lives to achieve. Until this is achieved your soul is a provisional member of the kingdom of the soul.

The First Initiation sees the birth of Christ-like love in your heart chakra.[17] By this we mean the selfless love on which your soul is based. The previous work of character building and purification prepares your

---

17 **Chakras:** Energy centres in our bodies through which energy flows. There are seven key ones which align with your spine up through your body. Each has a specific colour and shape and is associated with a specific organ and emotions.

heart centre to be able to receive and hold this love. The heart chakra has been expanding with additional energy, enabling it to express this higher-level love.

By the time of the First Initiation, the soul has mastered the cravings of the flesh. When human consciousness controls the body, it often shows as cravings for food beyond what is needed to sustain the body and sexual yearnings beyond the need to perpetuate the species. Prior to the soul mastering the body, the human will be attracted to activities that stimulate the body. After this Initiation, physical appetites are relegated to their rightful place. It does not mean that all physical cravings go away at this Initiation. Such a state of consciousness does not occur until the Fourth Initiation.

The First Initiation has much to do with one's sex drive. There is a transfer of energy from your sacral chakra to your throat chakra. Here the energy is used to express creative ideas governed by the soul. At this stage the desire for sex is not completely subdued. The transfer of energy from the sacral chakra can cause challenges in your life, especially when the transfer oscillates rather than remaining constant.

It is at this stage you start to realise the esoteric meaning of human sexuality. Sexual intercourse is a reflection of the soul interacting with the personality. It is part of the story of duality and synthesising of them to become one.

Following the First Initiation there is a strong yearning to serve. You recognise and experience the oneness of humanity, resulting in a commitment to living your life for the betterment of humanity. A sense of wanting to be part of the team helping in the evolution of human consciousness arrives. Your contribution will vary according to the ray you belong to and your karmic situation.[18] However you choose to serve, your life will be much less selfish than before Initiation.

---

18 **Ray:** In the Esoteric Wisdom each soul belongs to one of seven rays. Each ray has specific qualities their souls demonstrate, along with responsibilities to contribute to the evolution of humanity's consciousness in a specific way. A fuller description on the Seven Rays can be found in chapter 6.

Second Initiation

The number of incarnations between the First and Second Initiations can be considerable. To undertake the Second Initiation the soul must demonstrate that it has mastery over the emotional body. This is a crucial step but not an easy one to achieve.

The Second Initiation: the soul must demonstrate mastery over the emotional body.

Generally, today, the consciousness of humanity is largely directed by human emotions and the desires and wants they drive. Though mastery of the mind is developing, for most humans it is emotions that hold sway. Thinking and feeling are very different. But underlying subtle emotions can still influence the direction of your thoughts. For this reason, it can be easy to believe you have met the conditions of the Second Initiation, only to find that it is not the case.

Emotions drive our likes and dislikes, so they have influence over most areas in your life. Learning to discern between thinking and subtle emotions that affect your thoughts is key before you can move towards the Second Initiation.

At the Initiation you must demonstrate detachment from emotional experiences. Therefore, it is no surprise that the Initiation always involves a major emotional crisis in your life, which may be protracted over a number of years. To achieve the Second Initiation requires reflection on your emotional actions and reactions. Emotions have traditionally controlled thinking, but this needs to change if you want to move forwards to the Second Initiation.

Between the First and Second Initiations, you will gain a greater understanding of the spiritual nature of yourself and the purpose of your soul. However, as the emotional body is not yet fully mastered, over-enthusiasm can result. At the Second Initiation your soul must demonstrate that it is free from being a slave to ideas of the mind viewed as profoundly true and meaningful to life. These ideas can come to control the mind rather than the other way around. Mental obsession can become an issue, stopping the soul from moving forwards. This must be overcome to move on to the Second Initiation.

While disassociating with feelings, the soul is also developing higher emotions within consciousness such as feelings of compassion. A deeper level of calling to serve at a global level emerges and the sense of the importance of an inner group.

Today most students of Esoteric Wisdom and the evolution of human consciousness are generally found between the First and Second Initiation. An opening of the heart has occurred and a measure of control and leadership over the human physical body has been achieved. The challenge now is to rise above the emotions, and its desires, wants and influence over thinking.

Third Initiation

The Third Initiation is pivotal, as it is here that the soul gains leadership and control over the whole of the personality. At this stage the soul is fully infused into the personality and the conscious sense of self is that of the soul. The Third Initiation is when the duality of the soul and personality are fused into one.

The Third Initiation: the soul gains control over the whole personality.

By the Third Initiation, the initiate is able to discern between a thought, the thinker and the process of thinking. The mind is now thus the servant of the soul. The initiate knows himself experientially as transcendent to thought and thinking. The soul now knows it represents the mind of God within every human.

At the Third Initiation sacrifice is dominant. There emerges a willingness to sacrifice all in service of the greater whole (God). No longer does the thought of separateness deceive the initiate, and he becomes conscious of his participation in the life of the whole, a familiarity with his inner master is recognised, and his responsibilities to the ashram of the ray he belongs to become known.[19] All is then sacrificed to that responsibility.

The world as a whole is now viewed as the scope of service, as you now know humanity is one. Being well travelled and widely known

19 **Ashram:** In Esoteric Wisdom an ashram *is a place of spiritual guidance and support*. Esotericism doesn't define it as having an external location. Each ray has its own ashram.

doesn't make you a third-degree initiate. To be a third-degree initiate, the scope of your service will have positive worldwide ramifications. At the moment there are very few souls at this level of development, although their numbers are growing.

The initiate is now able to *consciously* sense their monad, the spark of Spirit in each of us. The first fleeting glimpse occurs at the moment of initiation. It is a very different consciousness from all that you have experienced before. You have a sense of being a part, yet also the whole, simultaneously.

Through many lifetimes the soul has aspired to reach the state of a third-degree initiate, to be fully living as soul. There is no need to strive to achieve this any longer. The third eye has opened even wider, and the initiate is now able to create loftier thoughts on evolution more effectively, giving them inner sight, wisdom and authority. Through this they can create ideas and actions which support the plan for humanity's evolution.

At this initiation the initiate receives an enormous influx of energy, so the energy body must be pure enough to support it.

Fourth Initiation

After the Third Initiation there is a rapid accumulation of spiritual knowledge. This is because the wisdom held by the soul is being synthesised into the intuition of the initiate. There is a profound realisation of the deeper mysteries of existence. The 'Plane of Intuition' is where the wisdom of divinity is found. The fourth-degree initiate finds that this is where their resting consciousness is centred.

The Fourth Initiation: full comprehension of immortal beingness.

The most notable feature of the Fourth Initiation is the destruction of the soul, which acts as the repository of your personal wisdom gained with such hard work over many lifetimes. You have strived to live your life through your soul and have viewed it as eternal. But now it is no longer useful in your onward development and must be destroyed. At the Fourth Initiation, the initiate realises the eternal consciousness is your Monad, not your soul. As the soul disintegrates, the initiate is free to uplift to their monad. This can be a distressing experience. This renunciation of the soul is reflected in the outward life of the initiate. Often the person must give up all that is humanly valued – friends, money, status – which can be very painful. Jesus took this Initiation at his crucifixion and demonstrated the level of sacrifice that is required. However, we should remember that it is the causal body that contains the soul's consciousness that is destroyed. Your consciousness and sense of self rises towards your Monad. From the Third Initiation the experience of the Monad is held, but at the moment of the soul being sacrificed, the view of the Monad is blocked and thus there is no reassurance as the initiate moves forwards and there is a dreadful feeling of being alone. The outer life feels meaningless and the initiate must demonstrate complete reliance on their own inner wisdom without any support. The initiate must prove there are no dependencies or fear before the upward journey to the Monad.

It is at this Initiation all karma must have been released. After the Fourth Initiation reincarnation is no longer mandated and the light of the Monad once again emerges. Death is fully understood to be an illusion. The initiate fully comprehends their immortal beingness.

•••

As we have mentioned earlier, Andrea's Awakening happened in her life as a neolithic farmer trudging along behind a plough in the mud when she had a thought about the meaning of life. Over the 5,000 years since then she has been on the path continuing to develop her own capabilities, some of which reflect the behaviours outlined in the stages of initiation. Perhaps one of her life experiences resonates with you?

Humans have not changed much in 5,000 years. For example, an abused wife in ancient times is not so different from one in modern times. See Andrea's life in that situation as a demonstration of a lesson needing to be learnt to define personal boundaries and not to allow others to cross them. It may help to appreciate that it is all right to say, 'I am kind to myself and I will not allow someone else to abuse me.' Andrea took several lives to learn and demonstrate this promise to herself.

Chapter 8: Learning about You and How You Might Help Yourself

Life is full of choices. I no longer believe life just happens. Each of you is very much in control of your lives by the choices you make – including indecision, where you give your choice and control of your life over to someone else. With this understanding you gain the opportunity to live many lives within one physical life. Each one is a better version of yourself. You trigger this simply by consciously choosing a new and higher set of life values. These will challenge you if you really want to live by them.

> ***A better version of you is triggered by choosing a new and higher set of life values.***

Andrea: I chose 'honesty'. That sounds simple. But I found that to be honest with myself and all my dealings with other people and institutions was indeed not simple. During the pandemic of 2020, when there was much uncertainty in the world, I chose to practice honesty, albeit kindly, and to encourage others to be honest with me. It was my attempt to help to bring more stability into those lives I touched. They could rely on me to do what I said I would do without a spin on it.

My experience was that although I thought of myself as a reasonably honest person, actually being honest consistently is much harder than I thought it would be. When I observed myself, I found that I did not speak the total truth all of the time. I realised that I was placing an emphasis in my communications that showed me in a better light, and I found I had to correct myself. Or rather, my soul highlighted my inaccuracies, which I needed to correct if I wanted to truly live my promise to myself of being honest. I had to improve my behaviour with others, including bodies such as the Tax Office and organisations from whom I had bought a service. This was not always easy.

I also held others to account in being honest in their dealings with me. This gave me some challenges with a builder who was doing some work for me. He found me a challenging customer, but I was not asking him to do anything more than he had said he would do, both verbally and in a contract. I do wonder if he learnt anything from the process he went through with me. I hope it gave him food for thought.

Going forwards in the current iteration of my best me, I have chosen the following life values to live by:

- Honesty.
- Kindness to self and others.
- Peacefulness in my person and those I interact with.
- Actively listening to others.
- Maintaining a nonjudgemental stance towards others and towards situations.

I am practising these values in my everyday life. There are some challenges in there for me. Besides honesty, I am a great believer in kindness. I feel the more kindness you bring into the world, the more you will benefit in this world and the next. I believe kindness accelerates your spiritual development. It really is true that what goes around comes around, so that if you smile at the world, it will smile back. Following these principles brings a greater sense of inner contentment and can make a considerable difference to the transformation of other people you encounter. I don't always get it right, but I am striving to improve my performance.

> *'Andrea is one of those rare people who not only say they believe in 'compassion and kindness of the highest order', but they actually live it and show it to you, too.'*
>
> – Elizabeth, Reading, UK

Guidance on the Life Values You Can Choose From

Alison: If you decide to re-examine your life values, here is a list of twelve life values you could choose from, in alphabetical order with their definitions:

1. **Compassion:** The feeling that arises when you are confronted with another's suffering and feel motivated to relieve that suffering.
2. **Courage to do the right thing:** You can know what the right thing to do is in a particular situation, but it can take courage to do it as there can be challenges involved in doing the right thing. Examples of those challenges might be disapproval from another person, fear of the outcome, or concern about the response from someone else.
3. **Gratitude:** The quality of being thankful, a readiness to show appreciation for and return kindness. Gratitude is one of many positive emotions. It's about focusing on what is good in your life and being thankful for the people and things in your life. Gratitude is pausing to notice and appreciate the things that we often take for granted, like family and friends and having a place to live and food to eat,
4. **Honesty:** If you describe someone as honest, you mean that they always tell the truth, and do not try to deceive people or break the law. Honesty is a facet of moral character that suggests positive attributes such as integrity, truthfulness, straightforwardness, including straightforwardness of conduct, along with the absence of lying, cheating and theft. Honesty involves being trustworthy, loyal, fair and sincere.
5. **Humility:** The quality of having a modest or low view of one's importance. Humility is the recognition and acceptance of reality through open-mindedness to truth. Humble leaders grasp their own capabilities in relation to others and the situation at hand.
6. **Integrity:** The quality of being honest and having strong moral principles. Having integrity means doing the right thing in a reliable way. It's a personality trait that many admire, since it means a person has

a moral compass that doesn't waver. It literally means having 'wholeness' of character, just as an integer is a 'whole number' with no fractions.

7. **Keeping promises to self and others:** To do what you say you will do. Whether the commitment is to yourself or to someone else, making a promise is a commitment that you will keep your word. It is a commitment that reinforces trust.
8. **Kindness:** The quality of being friendly, generous and considerate. The meaning is in how you choose to show it, be it through empathy, acceptance, kind gestures, thoughtfulness. Being kind is doing intentional, voluntary acts of kindness.
9. **Listening:** Take notice of and act on what someone says, and responding to advice or a request. When listening, one is hearing what others are saying and trying to understand what it means.
10. **Loving yourself:** Regard for one's own well-being and happiness. Self-love is a state of appreciation for oneself that grows from actions that support your physical, psychological and spiritual growth. Self-love means taking care of your own needs and not sacrificing your well-being to please others.
11. **Non-judgementalness:** Avoiding moral judgements. If a person or thing is non-judgemental, they do not judge or criticise. You are very close to being non-judgemental if you can accept a person exactly as they are, genuinely make no moral judgement about their situation, and empathetically try to get on their wavelength.
12. **Right compromise:** Settlement of differences reached by mutual concessions. It is often something intermediate between or blending qualities of two different things. When two people make a compromise, they essentially agree to meet in the middle. The importance of 'right' compromise is to ensure that the compromise is something you can live with and not feel you have had to compromise on your core values. This is a judgement call that only you can make for yourself.

These are the life values which I see people trying to put in place in their lives but sometimes struggle with. Below I have analysed Andrea's lives to identify life lessons she has grappled with in support of achieving each of these life values. It is work-in-progress for Andrea, so these life lessons are not exhaustive. Against each life lesson, I have identified the life it came from so you can locate and read the life again easily if you choose.

In reading this analysis, it might help you to understand what it means to adopt a particular life value and to assist you in choosing one that resonates with you.

Life Values and Supporting Life Lessons

1. **Compassion:**
   - Learning to uplift another person is good (Greek life, Classical Period).
   - We all make mistakes; it's part of the learning process (Greek Hellenistic Cyprus life).
   - Focus, concentration and practise enable you to achieve amazing things (Minoan life).
   - Compassion is a hard skill to learn but can enhance your response to situations and people greatly (Suffragette life).

2. **Courage to do the right thing:**
   - If you don't succeed the first time, try and try again until you do (Ancient Egyptian Crystal Pyramid life).
   - It is possible to build a new life even in very difficult circumstances (Greek life, Archaic Period).
   - A mother's desire to protect her child can be strong, enabling her to perform courageous acts (Greek life, Archaic Period).
   - Owning your mistake is the first step to overcoming it (Greek Hellenistic Cyprus life).
   - Sometimes it is better to let go of someone you love so they can choose to come back to you (Portuguese life).

3. **Gratitude:**
    - Knowledge imparted with love is remembered with love (Ancient Egyptian Crystal Pyramid life).
    - Difficult tasks become easier when you work as a team (Baptism life).
    - Love given and received is wonderful (Crete life).
    - Working in partnership enhances the experience and the outcomes achieved (Crete life).
4. **Honesty:**
    - Participating in a community is enriching to the soul (Whitby Abbey life).
    - Each of us is accountable for our own actions (Viking life).
    - Working through a challenge is often more rewarding than walking away from it (Viking life).
5. **Humility:**
    - All attempts to improve are good and should be encouraged (Fat man life).
    - Learning is fun and broadens your perspective on life and the world around us (Whitby Abbey life).
    - Working together providing mutual support is good (Cretan Life and Oracle).
    - Sometimes it's difficult to show someone you love them and want to please them (Jewish Prague life).
6. **Integrity:**
    - We are connected and influence all that is around us (Tibetan Monk life).
    - Our soul family loves and supports us through many lives (Greek Hellenistic Cyprus life).
    - Life should be balanced with both families and spiritual development (Roman Temple life).
    - Remember to share your spiritual journey with others to encourage them to join you in the journey of spiritual development (Roman Temple life).

7. **Keeping promises to self and others:**
   - Challenges often help us to learn a lesson about what we will allow to happen to us (Ancient Egyptian Temple life).
   - Be receptive to change, assess what is right for you and adopt the good elements (Oxyrhynchus Life).
   - Promises made before birth are for keeping (Irish Convent life).
   - Trust is important between people who love each other (US gold rush life).
8. **Kindness:**
   - A kindness offered at a time of challenge is remembered (Ancient Egyptian Temple life).
   - It is sometimes challenging to discern the difference between kindness and manipulation (Oxyrhynchus life).
   - Helping my community to thrive feels good (Glastonbury life).
   - Forgiveness can lighten the load for all involved (Suffragette life).
9. **Listening:**
   - Communicating in the right manner at the right time is important (Alchemist life, ancient Egypt).
   - Sometimes it's better to remain silent (Alchemist life, ancient Egypt).
   - Be more considered in your words (Greek life, Classical Period).
   - Learn not to dictate and be too pushy – give people time to assimilate the message (Greek life, Classical Period).
   - Understand the need to continually practise good communication to improve human interaction (Fat man life).
   - Good communication is important for a good relationship (Viking life).
10. **Loving yourself:**
    - Leading your life as you want to is true freedom and it uplifts your soul (Greek life, Archaic Period).
    - Learn to love and be kind to yourself (Fat man life).
    - You are never truly alone (Minoan life).

11. **Non-judgementalness:**
    - You love someone for who they are, not what they are (Cretan Life and Oracle).
    - Guides have a personality and sense of humour (Baptism life).
    - All attempts at developing yourself are good (Baptism life).
    - Love given unconditionally is returned unconditionally (Tibetan Monk life).
    - The definition of personal freedom is different for each of us (Spanish King's Librarian life).
12. **Right compromise:**
    - A constrained life does not necessarily mean it's a bad life. By being creative you can find joy in whatever is available to you (Spanish King's Librarian life).
    - Reinforcing the lesson to be flexible in life and to embrace the challenges it throws at you can transform your experience (Swiss Nun life).
    - Having the courage to say sorry is to be applauded (Suffragette life).

In all of this, I feel the art is to choose a few values and get used to them before you choose some more. I would recommend you choose one to three values. I chose one and found this a challenge! Try not to overload yourself.

Understanding the Wider Reality of Life

Research a number of viewpoints to gain a more rounded understanding of what spiritual development involves.

As you work on yourself and you recognise and come closer to the eternal part of yourself, it is sometimes challenging to understand what is happening to you. Andrea followed her intuition all along the way, but we worked together to gain a wider understanding from a range of the ancient and contemporary literature.

Brian Weiss's series of books on reincarnation and past life descriptions were an early influence in opening our minds to the possibility of living a number of lives and gaining wisdom through life experience and learning life lessons. Michael Newton and the various editions of *Journey of Souls* expanded on what we had learnt by adding the concept of a soul progressing through different stages. Also included is the grouping of souls almost into classes or teams in the After Life and the recognition of souls as energy, with colours reflecting experience and progress.

There are numerous descriptions of the kundalini experience and what it means to your energy body and consciousness. Most of us have not attained this level of development, but increasingly some people are doing so and offer service to assist the uplifting of humanity's consciousness so we might all live better lives.

Andrea and I have read many books and listened to lectures to gain a better understanding on human development. We came to the conclusion that Esoteric Wisdom gave us the most comprehensive guide, which is why I make good use of it here. The research gave us, I believe, a more rounded view of the topic, with the books by Brian Weiss and Michael Newton providing a gentle introduction which we could get our minds around. In all of this there is a danger of becoming overwhelmed. If you ever feel like this, stop your research and just follow your intuition. It is possible to be too much in your mind, rather than with your heart, where your real wisdom resides.

Use of Colour to Aid Understanding Intelligent Energy

Colour can be useful in gaining an understanding of the information that love, which is intelligent energy, is trying to bring you. Colour in a soul's energy is discussed in Michael Newton's books. Each of your chakras has a particular colour, which brings meaning to what capability that chakra brings you.

In creating a Soul Map you intuitively choose a colour to represent the members of your soul family – the souls you repeatedly reincarnate with over a number of lives. The colour will help to indicate the like-minded subgroups within your soul family and what capabilities they are helping you to learn. For example, if you are surrounded by blue members of your family, it is likely you are trying to improve your communication skills. My books *Creating a Soup Map* and *Finding Your Soul Family* address this subject in more detail. As an introduction to the meaning of colour when used with intelligent energy, a summary of the colours of your chakras and their meaning is included here.

Originating in Hinduism and Tantric Buddhism, chakras are energy centres in your body through which energy flows. There are seven key chakras, which align with your spine up through your body. Each has a specific colour and shape and is associated with a specific organ and emotions.

Let's take a look at each of the chakras:

Root Chakra. Found at the base of your spine in the tail-bone area. Red in colour, it is your foundation and addresses survival issues such as food and money.

Sacral Chakra. Found in the lower abdomen about two inches below the navel. Orange in colour, it is abundance, well-being, pleasure and sexuality.

Solar Plexus Chakra. Found in the upper abdomen. Yellow in colour, it is our ability to be confident and in control of our lives. It gives us our self-worth, self-confidence and self-esteem.

Heart Chakra. Found in the centre of the chest just above our heart. Green in colour, it is your ability to love. It gives you your love, joy and inner peace.

Throat Chakra. Found in the throat. Blue in colour, it gives you your ability to communicate, express your feelings and the truth.

Third Eye Chakra. Found in the forehead between the eyes. Indigo in colour, it is your intuition, imagination, wisdom, ability to think and make decisions.

Crown Chakra. Found at the very top of the head. Mauve in colour, it is your connection to spirituality, pure bliss.

A colour is attributed to each ray type in the Esoteric Wisdom and reflects the qualities of the ray. In knowing the ray you belong to, it will help you to identify the qualities to be found in your soul. As a person on the path, your soul will be influencing your life and the things you do. If you look back on your life you may well be able to see elements in your life which your soul has successfully influenced.

Astrological Influences on Your Current Life

Esoteric astrology is a soul-centred astrology. Less concerned with your outward personality or what's going to happen to you in this lifetime, esoteric astrology is about defining your soul's contribution to the evolution of humanity. The soul lives many lives, but the stars and planets' positions in the sky at the moment of your birth influences this life. It will indicate what your soul is seeking to achieve in this lifetime. The placement of Saturn at your time of birth is also an indication of which area in your life specific karma needs to be worked upon.

Andrea explored her esoteric astrological birth chart to gain a greater understanding of capabilities she was born with and the influences of the planets over this life.

Summary of Andrea's esoteric natal chart
Libra birth sign: At the soul level she seeks to find 'right-relationships'. Libra is

- The sign of counselling.
- Decisive and seeks to find the right decision based on a middle path. The negative side of Libra is to be indecisive or to rush decisions.
- More aware of duality and tries to lift your consciousness to a higher path where they fuse as one.
- Linked to Buddhism.
- Ruled by Venus, the sign of counselling.

Virgo rising sign: gateway to the soul and holds the soul's intention for this life. Virgo is

- Grounded and practical.
- Oriented toward hard work and detail.
- Precision – its negative side is perfectionism.
- The sign of the healer.
- The great spiritual sign of purification.
- Recognises the sacredness of your duality. Through the purification of the personality, the soul can bring itself out unencumbered in the service of humanity's upliftment.

Andrea as a Virgo/Libra

Andrea's Virgo soul is an advocate of healing and good form but is bringing it into the world with a Libra sensitivity to right relationships and capability to interface with people. Her soul seeks to help humanity to transform to achieve the right relationship between Mother Earth and the energy humanity utilises.

Pluto will help to shake things up and transform. Pluto rules the sign of Scorpio, which is the sign of psychology.

These are some of the approaches Andrea and I took to get to know ourselves. They are not the only ones available to you. Try whatever you are drawn to. Other approaches include shamanic journeying and lucid dreaming, to name but a few.

Part 3

What Can Humanity Look Forward To?

Chapter 9: Can We Achieve the Necessary Change to Uplift Humanity?

The key question is this: Is humanity globally where it should be for the move into the Aquarian Age and the upliftment of humanity's consciousness to live life in a different way as an enlightened species?

The answer is, quite possibly yes.

There is a 200-year overlap between the Piscean and Aquarian Ages. We are about halfway through this transition now. During the Aquarian Age the whole of humanity will be uplifted so that our consciousness knows, experiences and lives being connected to each other and with universal love. There is much work to be done to achieve this change. It is a significant challenge, but you need to remember that the Aquarian Age is predicted to last 2,160 years.

It takes 25 per cent of the population to accept a social change for the rest of the population to follow.

Typically, social change is driven by population growth and composition, culture and technology, the natural environment and social conflict. Social change is thus an ongoing process. It is often vocal minorities who initiate change. But it takes a threshold level of 25 per cent of the population to accept a social change, to influence the rest of the population to follow. The majority will adopt the new behavioural norm introduced by the minority.

On the surface, we may not notice social change. It can take many years, even hundreds of years, to make change happen, and only when you pause to look back do you see the scale of the change. Look at the change from just before World War I to the turn of the millennium. We have moved from horse-drawn carriages to cars, public health care, space travel and personal digital devices for communications. The life you lead now is vastly different from the life you would have lived in 1910.

Currently the instability in the world is creating a 'burning platform' for change. In this context a burning platform is the reason for and driver pushing people to decide that change is required for them to get to a better place where they can enjoy their lives more.

In going through this change to uplift humanity, there are three categories of people:

- **Those in denial of the need to change the way they live.** Most of humanity is in this category. The world's total population is in the order of 7.75 billion, and the size of this group is around 5.8 billion. This group will need assistance in making the change necessary in the Aquarian Age.
- **Those beginning to appreciate that we need to live our lives differently.** This is an increasingly larger group. This is the group that needs to reach 25 per cent of the world's population, circa 1.95 billion people, to make change happen. That is more than the population of the US and China combined, giving you an idea of the scale of the change needed. If you are reading this book, you are probably in this group. This group of souls are highly likely to make and sustain the change in behaviours before the end of the Piscean Age.
- **Those awakened to the need for change and living it now.** This group is relatively small compared to the whole population of humanity. These souls have returned to Earth at this time to help humanity to uplift its consciousness.

It will need 25 per cent of the world's population, 1.95 billion people for the upliftment of humanity to happen. This is more than the population of the US and China combined.

In this world today there are empowered people holding the new state of consciousness to allow an emergence of the next state of human consciousness. They are the people of the future here today.

This is an exciting time to be alive on Earth. Many changes are already happening, and Andrea and I are trying to make our contributions to those changes. I hope you would like to do the same.

Modern World Challenges: Creating the Platform for Change

There is much instability in the world at the moment. This is undermining peoples' feelings of security and threatening their ability to manage their lives to ensure that they and their families can live safe and happy lives. Examples of this include:

- **The Pandemic of 2020.** This was like a great pause button for humanity. The pace of life slowed as people were constrained in their homes and had to fall back onto basic everyday living. The noise humans make was greatly reduced, with less car movement, no planes and few trains. Even in cities you could now hear the birds singing. Uncertainty and the vulnerability of the elderly and people living with chronic illnesses brought the best out in people. People volunteered to food-shop for and assist those who could not leave their homes. Although the situation was traumatic, it brought the best out in people, with strangers helping one another to help make the situation more manageable. There was a greater sense of community between neighbours, where perhaps before there had been little connection with one another. There has been social change as a result, perhaps due to the length of time new ways of living had to be practised. Working from home is now technically more possible and socially more acceptable. This has released many people from living in cities if they do not have to commute every day of the working week. Technology played a key role in keeping people in contact with one another, both for business and social reasons. This has continued afterwards, making international contact much easier with the use of video systems to create a greater sense of being together even if you are many miles apart. This is helping families and businesses to continue to be more connected.

- **War in Ukraine, 2022.** This conflict began soon after the pandemic, and I feel this made people much more compassionate about another people's situation. As Ukrainian people fled the war in their country, movement across country boundaries was made possible, albeit with some administration problems. People opened their homes to Ukrainians who had nowhere to live. Ukraine provides the world with food, particularly cereals, and their invader, Russia, provides energy and has used energy as a weapon against European countries to try to control their reaction to the invasion of Ukraine. All of this has highlighted to people how interconnected we are on a physical level, which then ripples into our sense of feeling safe and secure.
- **Sustainability of the environment.** Humanity as a collective share the planet we live on. If we care for the planet, it can be a beautiful place to live for future generations. If we abuse it, it will become an increasingly sterile and ugly place to be and ultimately would be unable to sustain life. Increasingly there are movements lobbying for more sustainable ways to live, including drives to eliminate polluting methods of providing energy such as burning fossil fuels and using petrol in cars. It is a start in changing humanity's attitudes and therefore actions in relation to the planet, but I do wonder if it is enough, or fast enough. It feels as if the 21st century is a pivotal one for discovering new ways of living to protect the very place we live.

Chapter 10: Esoteric Wisdom: The Tibetan's Prophesies for the 21st Century

Alice Bailey's books were written between 1919 and 1949. They include esoteric thought and cover a range of topics, including how spirituality relates to the solar system, healing, meditation and human spiritual evolution. She states that they were telepathically channelled to her by a Master of Wisdom known as the Tibetan.

Much has been written about Alice Bailey's books and how authentic they may be. You can indeed make your own decision on them. However, there is an increasing interest in the texts and the thoughts conveyed by the Tibetan. Throughout these texts, the key themes are honesty and being of service to others for the uplift of humanity. To me, these feel like good objectives for my own life, and I have valued the insight, guidance and challenges these books have brought me.

A small group of spiritually minded friends could already see change commencing in each of the key areas.

I was fortunate enough to observe a small group of spiritually minded friends discussing the Tibetan's prophesies for the 21st century, which were made more than seventy years ago. Their discussion highlighted their observations of where they could already see change commencing in each of the key areas. It surprised me how much of the prophesies are already coming to fruition in the first quarter of the 21st century. This group included a retired anaesthesiologist, an artist and psychic medium, and an energy healer.

The Arts

Beginning in 2025, there will be a revolution in artistic expression not seen since the Renaissance Period. Art will again focus on uplifting the human spirit. Humanity will learn the 'art of living in order to produce synthesis and beauty'.

A new form of singing will emerge and become widely used. It has a new form of breathing to make sounds that have deep spiritual resonances.

Discussion

- Some members of the group had experienced Jill Purce's overtone singing, which sounds like angelic bells rising from a chant and takes you deep within. Jill lives in London and holds workshops internationally to increase awareness of the voice as a spiritual, meditative and healing tool that all of us possess but most no longer use.

A new form of singing will emerge and become widely used.

- At Sacred Acoustics, Karen Newell has developed the digital creation of sacred harmonics: digital harmonic frequencies and other sound effects are woven and layered together to entrain the brain to a theta state, supporting creativity, intuition, learning and stress reduction. Karen Newell and Eben Alexander, a neuro-surgeon from the US and bestselling author of *Proof of Heaven*, believe that ultimately direct experience is key to fully realising how we are all connected through the binding force of unconditional love and its unlimited ability to heal. They travel the world sharing the experience of using sacred acoustics to connect with unconditional universal love.
- Art and music, plus other creative activities, should be experienced by all in our growing up years. Sadly, in recent years the time allocated to the arts in schools has become more limited. Schools need to appreciate the value of the arts in developing the whole person, rather than just to pursue the development of the mind. During creative activities, many people naturally connect with their own soul and/or Universal Energy. It is an important experience to have at an early age and promotes its practice later in life.

Science

A radical discovery will be made which will entirely change the means by which humanity will utilise electricity. A great discovery will be made on the use of light and the directive power of thought. Some of the significant mysteries of light will be solved. This will enable development of new scientific instruments capable of being directed by the human eye and the power of focused thought.

> ***A great discovery will be made on the use of light and the directive power of thought.***

There will be astronomical discoveries which show that our solar system has 115 planetary bodies in orbit around the sun. These discoveries will be made as a result of emerging capabilities for some people to see energy and thus prove that there are many planets manifested down to etheric matter rather than as far as dense physical form.

Science will prove the existence of the soul.

Discussion

- Already prosthetics have been developed which respond to a person's thoughts rather than using a mechanical control mechanism. This can be life-enhancing for someone who has lost a limb, enabling them to live a fuller life.
- Psychic mediums are the forerunners of the power of focused consciousness as they live their lives daily using energy and focused thought to receive guidance from Spirit.
- Reiki, and energy healing more generally, is about the practitioner connecting with Universal Energy and channelling it on behalf of the patient. However, unlike conventional medicine, the patient's body and soul chooses how much of the healing it wants to take.
- Some of the group can already see energy as different colours in their mind's eye.

In science in particular, the group had concerns that these wonderful discoveries for the betterment of humanity could be abused and used for control or war. Artificial Intelligence and robotics were of particular concern.

Healing Arts

By the end of the 21st century the majority of the population will understand that death is non-existent as it is currently understood. Advanced members of humanity will have demonstrated 'continuity of consciousness' and be able to be in both worlds at the same time. Scientific control of the death process will be developed to help people through the death experience.

The majority of the population will understand that death is non-existent as it is currently understood.

Music and sound will be increasingly used therapeutically to help people to heal. A new form of music will emerge for this purpose.

Discussion

- Psychic mediums are the forerunners of being able to reach beyond the veil to share messages from loved ones who have passed. However, the group felt that the space between those on Earth and those in the After Life is narrowing. It is almost as if the bridge between the two is strengthening. You have only to speak to bereaved people to know that loved ones try very hard and do succeed in sending a sign or message to grieving loved ones. It does show that everyone is capable of connecting and communicating across the perceived divide.
- Already we are seeing examples of well-known people from the spiritual community who have passed and chosen to reconnect with people on Earth. An example of this is available on the Humanity Team's website with Wayne Dyer and his daughters.

Chapter 11: Practices to Aid Living Your Best life and Awakening to Your Soul

What can you do to aid your own development and thereby contribute to Humanity's consciousness uplifting?

It's as simple as just being the best version of yourself you can be. This will evolve over time as experiences, studying and possibly memories aid you to be a better next version of yourself. If this approach is not concrete enough for you and you would like practices and processes to consider, here are seven key ones to consider.

Seven Practices to Help Start You on Your Way

1. **Step back and observe yourself.**
   Go within to a space of inner peace and hear the wisdom of your soul. You don't need to remember past lives. Ask yourself what your natural talents are. What life lessons are you trying to learn?

   The simplest way to find your inner peace is to go for a walk in nature with only yourself. Even in a city you can find green spaces. Look at the green grass, the beautiful trees and the dynamic, changing sky or a wonderful sunset. As you admire the beauty which is all around you, you will absorb the soothing energy of Mother Nature. Breathe deeply and take that energy within you. Your own energy will respond and relax. You don't have to try to do it, it just happens naturally.

As you feel your energy relaxing, so your calmness will arrive. It is a calmness deep within you. Go to that spot deep inside where your calmness sits. It is in that place where you can most easily connect with your soul and converse.

Your soul is a kind, objective and wise observer of your life. Your soul will give you the guidance you seek. Your guidance will always be positive and uplifting. Your soul will aid you even in the most difficult of circumstances and guide you to find the best of you to respond.

2. **Respond rather than react.**
   When you react in the moment it is instinctual and therefore most likely not from your highest viewpoint. Pause for a second and consider your response before you give it. If time allows, take three deep breaths in through your nose and out through your mouth. We spoke about connecting with your intuition on page 49 in chapter 2.

   Connecting with your intuiton doesn't have to be obvious to anyone else. Many people place their hand on their heart to aid this connection. Connecting with your intuition and placing your hand on your heart will enable you to speak from the wisdom of your heart. People will hear the honesty and authenticity of what you say.

   I can assure you that your response will come from a higher viewpoint. People will respond accordingly, and it will be more effective in moving the situation and your life forward.

> *'When someone more senior than me was agitated or cross with me, while they were ranting, I would take three deep breaths right into my heart and then place my hand on my chest. I am sure this helped me to connect with my soul, who would then share their wisdom on the situation and help me to frame a reply. It also helped me to display that I had the patience to* listen *to the person and was willing to collaborate to resolve the issue. I found the response to my reply was generally positive, so I can only assume I gave the best reply I could in the situation. It definitely helped my work life.'*
>
> – Vicki, Oxford, corporate manager

At times of stress, we all look for people or things to help us, be it at work or at home. You can always create a Soul Map,[20] which highlights the important people in your life and the life lessons you are trying to learn and helps you to connect with your soul for guidance. Creating a Soul Map provides insight into your life. People who have done this, I notice, often keep one on their desk at work and/or in their kitchen at home. These are two places where difficult but important conversations seem to happen. The Soul Maps may be different if different people and life lessons are involved.

3. **Follow your passions.**

Be your best self and feel joy within. When you follow your passions, which are often promptings from your soul, somehow you really enjoy it and doors just seem to open for you. Some people call it being in the flow of life. It is just the right thing for you and your life at that moment in time.

As you practice this more the joy becomes more sustained. It will radiate out from you and start to affect those around you. One of my favourite four-minute meditations to aid feelings of joy: 'Reflection for Joy'.

You can scan this QR code to access this meditation.

4. **Be part of the change in humanity.**

It is wonderful to be alive when humanity is being given the opportunity to step into the next phase of our development. This comes with its own challenges, but you also can make a contribution to the change by living your best life. Remember, as we said before, to make a change to living by higher values, it takes 25 per cent of the population to be actively trying to do so. Once 25 per cent of us are doing it, the rest will follow over time. This is not a change our political or national leaders will dictate to us to do. This change is one that is happening at

20 **Soul Map:** A high-level process available in *Creating Your Soul Map*; a more detailed use of Soul Maps is found in *Finding Your Soul Family*, also by Alison Wem.

a personal level, with you and me making our own decisions on how we wish to live.

Following your energy is part of the spiritual path of development. Wherever you can contribute to humanity and the change we are experiencing, know that it is part of your own development as well. Find whatever suits you and your life.

My husband took to doing food shopping for people who were incapacitated and couldn't get to the shops in the pandemic of 2020. In the early days I think he valued having a legal reason to leave home during the lockdowns of 2020/21, but he came to enjoy helping these people. They became a part of his life, and they both enjoyed seeing each other and often had a good chat as well as getting the food shopping done. In addition to food shopping, he is now taking beloved pets to the vets, collecting prescriptions and doing many other errands. My observation was that the service he provided added value to his own sense of well-being and a more joyful life as much as the people he was helping. It was most definitely a win-win.

5. **Consciously choose the life values you wish to live by.**
As I mentioned earlier, in 2020 I decided to live an honest life in all I say and do. I observed myself and I was really upset to see that I wasn't totally honest all the time. I could hear myself say something, and then another part of me said, 'That is not quite correct' and I had to stop and correct myself. It seems that the art to this type of change is to step back and connect with your inner observer. It will give you feedback on your performance in living your chosen life value. It is well-meant feedback, so try not to get frustrated or feel cross with yourself when you make a slip. Just correct yourself, and over time it will seem to feel more natural until you do it without consciously thinking about it.

Imagine the difference it would make to all of us if we could rely on each other doing what we say we will do? And if it is not possible, to come back and say so and explain why it's not possible. Trust in each other would become a natural way of being.

There are many other values you can sincerely consider adopting, such as compassion, tolerance, kindness and giving service to others. They are outlined in more detail in chapter 8. I felt it was too hard to adopt all of them at once, so I chose honesty to practice first. My experience was that after a while some of the other values just followed naturally.

6. **What gifts have you inherited from your bloodline and culture?** Andrea's examples included:

    - A great-great-grandad from the Glastonbury area in the UK who was a master stonemason and was greatly attracted to Andrea's exploration of scrying stones for messages.[21]
    - She discovered many of her family are natural psychic mediums and healers, and in their rural community in living memory were often called upon when an animal was ill and the vet was unable to help.
    - The Glastonbury area was an outpost of the Atlanteans. With the fall of Atlantis, they found themselves stranded. Almost inevitably, they inter-bred with the locals, causing some of their skills to be passed down the bloodline. In the west country of England where Andrea's family are based, her family is very accepting of and integrated with the old ways and skills.

Try doing some research into your family. I have found older people often love to chat about what it was like in times gone by and how earlier generations lived. It is good to gather this information before it is lost through older family members passing. Now is a good time to start this discovery work. Of course, the internet, books and media can enrich your personal story and the gifts from your family.

Consider the culture you were raised in. It can bring good, positive influences to your life. Even if you do not agree with how lives were

21 **Scrying:** The practice of looking at a stone with focused consciousness to detect messages or visions.

lived historically, you will at least take a considered view and live your life as you feel is right for you.

When a family has changed country historically, it is interesting to note how this might continue to influence your thinking and behaviour today. You can make conscious decisions on what your want to retain or leave behind. The art of it is to do so consciously rather than to just let it happen.

7. **Keep going and don't give up, as every little bit helps.**
   Change is never easy, and sometimes it feels as if you take two steps forwards and one back. This is normal and all part of being human. Don't give up at the latest hurdle. Spirit never gives you more than they know you can cope with. You just need to discover what is the best way of finding your way through a challenge and coping with what is presented to you. Taking control of your life and what you allow to happen to you, your life and your body is key to not feeling like a victim.

Taking control of your life and what you allow to happen to you, your life and your body is key to not feeling like a victim.

A good friend who was diagnosed with cancer at 33 years old felt very much the victim. Her chance of getting the cancer at that age was 0.5%. Yet here she was with it and struggling to find a way through the potential treatments. After grappling with the issue for a while, she decided to handle the situation by researching the treatments offered to her and their potential longer-term side effects. Fortunately, she had a background in health care, so she felt she could make informed decisions on what was right for her. She also used diet and alternative health practices to assist the more conventional medicines, and she was careful to ensure that they did not conflict with one another.

Now successfully in remission, my friend spends time and energy raising awareness on how young adults can find positive ways through cancer treatment. She is sharing the knowledge she gained on treatments in a way nonmedical people can understand. My friend is gaining traction with charities and the media with her messages, which are inspirational and offer a way forwards in what appears to be a desperate situation. First and foremost, my friend never gave up hope on herself. I am in admiration of her.

These seven practices will help you to consciously engage with your life. Life is a gift, and these practices will maximise what you learn during your life. Choose whichever ones feel right for where you are in your life today. Your soul will help you in your choices. One may jump out at you, or you will naturally be drawn to those which will be useful to your life. This is your soul gently prompting you.

For some people it can assist you in your endeavours if you consciously know and understand the fundamental drivers underlying your interests and views about life. What type of soul do you have that guides your interests?

Appreciating the ray your soul belongs to can help you to understand the qualities your soul brings to your life.

Explore the Seven Rays of Soul Types and Discern Your Soul Type

In the Esoteric Wisdom your soul belongs to a ray. Each ray has qualities which support the soul's purpose and destiny. Some of these qualities will be influencing what you are doing with your life. There is much literature online about the Seven Rays, but here is a summary. It might help you to determine if learning more about this topic would help you to understand yourself and your passions. If you seek to understand the Seven Rays in more detail, I would recommend reading William Meader's book *Shine Forth: The Soul's Magical Destiny*.

Appreciating the ray your soul belongs to can help you to understand the qualities your soul brings to your life. This may explain some of your behaviours and why you have made key choices on your career. The more you discover about yourself, the more you can use your qualities for the betterment of humanity and work towards delivering your purpose.

First Ray: Ray of Will and Power, colour red

A soul from the First Ray will seek to express their will to make change happen, to break down the barriers which tend to arrest humanity's evolution. They are purposeful in moving towards their objective and destiny. They tend to launch new and progressive ideas and initiatives in support of humanity's positive change. Typical job roles include leadership, government, CEOs and other executive roles.

Second Ray: Ray of Love and Wisdom, colour blue

Love and the wisdom achieved through understanding are the qualities of the Second Ray. The soul seeks to express uplifting thoughts using these qualities. These souls seek to unite people through uplifting transformational ideas and engendering working together. Their ability to relate to spiritual vision and to see the greater truth waiting to be revealed aids them. Typical job roles are teaching, counselling and the healing arts.

Third Ray: Ray of Active Intelligence, colour green

Intellect and the ability to see the interconnected nature of people and systems are the qualities expressed by a Third Ray soul. Intellectually resourceful and sensitive to profound ideas, these souls are often dedicated to finding innovative applications to new ideas by adapting new knowledge into designs that have functional value.

Fourth Ray: Ray of Harmony through Conflict, colour yellow

This soul is urged to reconcile and synthesise opposite perspectives to seek the sacred truth found within conflicting points of view. Doing so reveals the greater truth from synthesising both perspectives. Fourth Ray souls recognise that humanity is struggling to get to a higher and more peaceful state. They will seek to achieve right compromise to move from the old ways of living to the new ones.

Fifth Ray: Ray of Concrete Knowledge and Science, colour orange

This ray seeks to give clarity and accuracy to human thought and perception. Souls on this ray desire to discern what is true and what only seems true. Fifth Ray souls are typically analytical and ascertain truth through close study and investigation. These souls consider that intuition is an aid to the mind rather than an adversary.

Sixth Ray: Ray of Idealism and Devotion, colour rose

The souls of the Sixth Ray seek to help humanity to recognise the evolutionary value of ideals. They are driven to assist humanity's evolution by espousing ideals that are uplifting blueprints underlying divine ideas. Their destiny is to reveal to humanity that a heart-based ideal has the power to transform life both for the individual and in the collective. Their challenge is to express the good and beautiful without becoming fanatical.

Seventh Ray: Ray of Ceremonial Order, colour violet

A Seventh Ray soul is urged to give form to the formless truth. They seek to bring spiritual love and wisdom into practical everyday life. They feel a responsibility to engender the best of the human spirit in all we do. Seventh Ray souls tend to have good organisational skills to assist them in this endeavour. As humanity is entering a Seventh Ray age, the destiny of humanity is being shaped now by Seventh Ray souls. This is a unique opportunity for Seventh Ray souls.

Andrea: I believe I belong to the Second Ray: Ray of Love and Wisdom. Of course, this understanding could change over time as I increasingly get to know myself. But this ray feels right for me with my current understanding of myself. This is largely based on my desire to help others to understand something, to appreciate it and work with it no matter if it's a challenge or a joy. I am a healer and psychic medium. I aim for the individual to feel more uplifted after a session with me. When someone feels uplifted, I have observed that they cope better with whatever is presented to them in their life. It seems to help them to get in touch with a stronger and more knowing part of themselves who helps them with their life situation. When this happens, it is my reward for performing the roles I do.

Each soul retains its soul type throughout all their lives. However, the personality/ego type can change with different lives depending on what the soul is trying to achieve.

At any one time, there is a mix of soul types on Earth. The quantities of a particular soul type being incarnate will vary depending on the development needs of humanity. At the moment I believe there are significant numbers of Ray 2 souls to help educate humanity in the new ways of living. Ray 7 souls are stepping forward to assist in shaping humanity's progress.

Chapter 12: Death – The Taboo Subject

Andrea: In many cultures, particularly Western ones, death is a subject often not spoken of and consequently surrounded in fear. Other cultures deal with death better – for example, where wailing and crying are expected, allowing the mourners to express their emotions of loss at no longer having a loved one with them on Earth. This expression of what they are feeling helps to get the anguish out of their bodies, ultimately leading to a healthier mind and body. The 'stiff upper lip', where men are not meant to cry, is a far less healthy attitude. Of course, men feel emotions as keenly as women.

My first experience of the dying process came when I was eleven years old. All was calm and I was surrounded by a feeling of enormous love.

My first experience of the dying process happened when I was eleven years old, lying in bed with pneumonia and struggling to breathe with my body wracked in pain with each breath I took. I decided to explore what it would feel like to not try to take my next breath. To my surprise I didn't splutter like you do when your head is under water in a swimming pool and you need your next breath.

All was calm and I was surrounded by a feeling of enormous love that words cannot sufficiently describe. A loving guide explained that I had a choice over what happened next. I could step forwards, but once I had done so I wouldn't be able to return to my body. Alternatively, I could return. At that moment I heard Mum screaming and crying for me to come back. I could feel her anguish in her voice. I loved my mum and I didn't want to be the cause of her feeling so upset, so I made the decision to return. As soon as I had that thought, I was back in my body. However, I was changed by that experience, since I had learnt that death is not a process to be feared. You do have choice and are guided and loved all the way through it.

Death is not a process to be feared. You do have choice and you are guided and loved all the way through it.

At one period in my life, it seemed to be my destiny to hold the hands of the dying. Over a period of five years most of my close relatives passed and I was with them when they went through the process of dying. It included my dad, mother-in-law, husband, mum and even the family cat. My aunt slipped silently out of our lives and didn't need me to hold her hand. I really do not know why. Perhaps her links were stronger with her loved ones already in the After Life.

The first dead body I had ever seen was my father-in-law in his coffin. My late husband and I were on holiday when he was taken gravely ill. We made an extreme effort to be with him but sadly didn't get the opportunity to say goodbye. My husband wanted to see his dad one final time to help himself to gain closure and to fully realise his dad had passed. I didn't really want to see the body, but I didn't have the heart to let my husband go alone. When I looked at my father-in-law, I instantly sensed it was not him. He always had a lovely smile and was welcoming you into his home. This body, which had a face that looked like marble, wasn't him. Whatever the essence is that makes a person was gone. This body was like a set of clothes you might drop on the floor as you climb into bed. This body was not the person I loved.

When my dad realised he was terminally ill, it was a difficult time for all of us. No-one wanted to acknowledge that my dad had a limited time with us. We each carried that burden within us during our daily lives. In the end, I screwed up my courage and raised the subject of death. I explained my near-death experience and that dad did not need to fear the process as it was surrounded by love. I felt it was my mum who had the greatest challenge being left on Earth without the person she loved the most and had been married to for more than fifty years. My dad explained that it wasn't dying he was sad about but not being with my mum and caring for her. With the remaining time, he set about doing all he could to make life easier for her when he was gone. He bought a smaller car which she would find easier to drive, changed the central heating boiler, organised a gardener and finally arranged and paid for his own funeral. He had chosen his coffin, booked the wake and even listed the people he would like us to invite. Near to his death, he told me where the folder was with all the arrangements detailed in it. I was taken aback but thought that was so like my dad and loved him for it. He had done his best to surround his passing with his love for us.

I don't know where my mum got the strength from, but all through the dying process she gently spoke to her dying husband.

On the morning of his passing, Mum, my brother and I were all with him. This was the first time I had seen someone go through the process of dying. I don't know where my mum got her strength from, but all through the process she gently spoke to her dying husband. I think it was a comfort to all of us. My dad had been in a lot of pain, but at the moment of his passing, the tension in his face from the pain faded and he smiled one last big smile. I didn't feel he was smiling at us but at his own mum and dad, who had come to collect him and take him home. His life was a job well done but it was now over. My mum is naturally a psychic medium. After dad passed, whenever she had to do a practical job at home she used to consult him and ask him to tell her what she had to do. It worked; she did some amazing tasks.

There were challenges in the relationship between my late husband and his mother. When we received the call to say she had been taken ill and that we needed to come, my husband declined to go. My husband was an only child so I knew she would be on her own. I left my husband looking after our children and went to my mother-in-law. It turned out to be much more serious than we had thought. The hospital told me my mother-in-law didn't have long to live. Her nephew brought her sister, whom she was close to, to visit. I phoned my husband asking if he wanted to come, as later he might regret not speaking to her. He didn't make it in time.

I sat with my mother-in-law through the night. I tried talking to her, but she didn't realise she was dying and asked me to stop as she was tired and was trying to sleep. Near the end I tried to talk to her as my mum had done for my dad. I struggled to find the right words to say. I am not sure I was much of a comfort, but I did my best. I concluded that everybody's passing is different.

I didn't know if my husband could hear me but I wanted him to feel his departure was surrounded in love. Years later he came back to say he had heard me and my voice and my love were a great comfort to him.

When my husband was taken ill, the doctors fought all night to save him. I stood by his bedside all the time holding his hand and talking to him. At some point, he lost the will to live and drifted into a coma. He was transferred to intensive care to see if he and his body decided to stay with us. Sadly, they didn't and as the machines were turned off that were keeping him alive, I held his hand and talked to him, saying how much I loved him and wanted him in my life and our children's lives. I didn't know if he could hear me, but I wanted him to feel his departure was surrounded in love. Years later he came back to tell me he had heard me and my voice and my love were a great comfort to him.

With my mum's passing, she was in intensive care for some time in a coma before she decided to leave her body. My brother, uncle and I used to take it in turns to sit with her. When it was my turn, I sat by her bed with all the machines whirring around me. I didn't speak to my mum out loud; we spoke telepathically. I asked her how she was doing.

She gave me a picture of herself being in a rowing boat on a calm, misty river. The boat was secured to the riverbank by a long rope. The boat wasn't near the bank but out in the middle of the river with the mist swirling around it. My mum was sitting in the boat trying to decide whether to return to the riverbank and life on Earth or to drift off into the mist to the After Life. She was hesitating as she understood that if she returned, her body was now compromised and she would be unable to return to her old life. She wanted to go to the After Life to be with her husband, but she didn't want to leave me all alone without a husband. She had been an enormous help and comfort to me since my husband had passed. On the other hand, my mum realised I was a loyal daughter and would take her into my home to care for her in her newly disabled body. But caring for a disabled mother was not the life she wanted me to live. She sat in her boat between life and death trying to make her decision.

I reassured her I would find the strength to live my life alone and to raise my children. She should not allow my situation to cloud her decision. She should choose what was right for her. If she wanted to be with her husband and didn't like the thought of being disabled, it was all right by me. All she had to do was to let go of the rope. My mum passed a few hours later.

Death is not something to be feared. It is but a transition from one realm to another. You are not your body, the essence of you survives death and you are able to stretch across from one realm to another to speak with and comfort loved ones.

The first year after my mum's passing was the worst year of my life. I hit a low point and had to learn to go deep within to haul myself out of the pit in which I found myself. However, the human spirit is very strong, and I did eventually rebuild my life. The thing I missed most was physical human contact. I craved a hug from someone. Of course, my children loved and hugged me. But I wanted an adult's hug from a body the same size as me. Such is the taboo and embarrassment around death that friends in our village would cross the road when they saw me and wave from a distance as they didn't know what to say to me. This summarised the West's approach to death and grieving.

My mum came back and gave me a physical hug.

My mum realised that I was struggling, and when I was dozing one day she came back and gave me a physical hug. She was absolutely delighted that I had felt it. It had been something she wanted to do but she had to learn a lot in the After Life to be able to do it. The experience was a delight to both of us and I felt wonderfully close to my mum again.

Shortly after this our family cat was ailing. My daughter was distraught at the thought of losing yet another person from our family. There was nothing I could say that would calm her. In the end we took the cat into the warm sitting room and made him comfortable. I made up camp beds on the floor and my daughter and I rested beside him all night so he would not be alone. In the morning my guide said to me: 'Your cat has spent his last night on Earth.'

Unusually, he used words rather than telepathic communication. I can only assume he wanted to make sure I had understood him. The vet said there was nothing we could do. With a lot of drugs, he might live a compromised life for a while. It would be kinder to let him go. To my surprise, my daughter said he would not enjoy a confined life indoors and that we should let him go. So my daughter had made our decision, and we sat with him while he passed. On that day my daughter was stronger than me and I loved her for it. Life does give you surprises. I did wonder why I seemed destined to sit with the dying and hoped my daughter had not taken on my burden.

This was the last passing I experienced for some years.

From this phase of my life, I experienced death at first hand. I still agreed with what I had said many years before to my dad: it is harder on those left behind on Earth. It is not an easy school to learn in. A friend said to me recently that after her dad passed her mother said to her, 'It felt so final, the parting from my husband.'

The distance between the After Life and Earth is becoming less and the bridge between the two realms is getting stronger.

But it doesn't need to be or feel like that. With the move from the Piscean Age towards the uplifting of humanity's consciousness in the Aquarian Age, I believe the distance between the After Life and Earth is becoming less and the bridge between the two realms is getting stronger. If you speak to the bereaved, it never ceases to amaze me how people who have passed try their hardest to send you messages. Mostly they are not words but a sign of some sort, a knowing, like the jumping out of the words of a song on the radio which are meaningful to you. My sole driver for learning to be a psychic medium was to learn the language of Spirit, and to be able to bridge the gap between the After Life and life on Earth, to communicate with passed loved ones. It took nine years for my late husband and I to communicate. You can imagine how excited I was when it happened. My late husband became quite known to my friends in the psychic mediumship circle I sat in. He used to join us in class and try to help us trainee mediums to communicate with passed loved ones. He even came with the late husband of a member of our circle and spoke on his behalf as he seemed unable to speak for himself. Our teacher was surprised but delighted, as was I.

You are not your body – the essence of you survives death.

Miracles do happen and increasingly so as humanity starts to appreciate our capabilities are much greater than we have realised historically. Death is but a transition. It is a natural process and not one to be feared. Our loves and lives continue beyond death.

A long-standing friend who is approaching ninety years old has this to say on death:

> *'People are often afraid of death, but they need not be. Loved ones should aim to help make the passing easy and peaceful. This is not always the case although I rather feel it is from ignorance rather than intent.*
>
> *'My friend Shirley, who is a healer, received a message that her good friend Tim was gravely ill in hospital and not expected to see the end of the day. She asked me to go with her to the hospital. When we arrived, we found Tim propped up in bed looking agitated with his relatives surrounding his bed. They were in an anxious state and not wanting him to pass.*
>
> *'Shirley asked the relatives to leave. Tim immediately said: 'Thank goodness you are here.'*
>
> *'Tim had been unable to pass while he could feel his loved ones' strong desire for him to stay on Earth. Shirley went over to Tim, and his agitation reduced and his face relaxed. She placed her hand on his back at the base of his neck. His whole body relaxed and I saw a bright white light as his soul gracefully rose up above his head and went onwards back to Spirit.*
>
> *'It was Tim's desire to return to Spirit, but he had felt locked in to staying by his loved ones not wanting to let him go. When he was able to relax, his soul took action and returned home. It was a lovely and peaceful passing thanks to Shirley.'*
>
> – Paula, London

Whatever the essence is that makes a person was gone. This body was not the person I loved.

It is not uncommon to feel the soul leaving as someone passes. It is more unusual to see the soul leaving, but if seen it is not usually spoken about. Such is the West's approach to death. This is a shame, as to see the soul is a beautiful experience. In the West Country, in England, where Andrea's family are from, it is an old tradition to leave the doors and windows open when someone is approaching death to make the soul's exit easier. There was more understanding of the dying process historically when people were closer to nature and the universe. We have lost some of this as we moved into the more modern age of science.

If you are still feeling anxious about death, there is one last thing I would like to say to you. Each time you go to sleep at night, you are practising the death process. A part of you withdraws from your body and goes to a place for love and guidance. Dreams can be a wisp of a memory of your night-time activities. On wakening you return to your body to live your next day. You do this each day of your life.

You only ever pass when the time is right for you.

In sleep you retain a link to your body and you can return to it very rapidly if you need to. In the death process I believe you let go of this link and effectively the link between your consciousness and body is broken. You only ever do this when the time is right for you. It is your soul that makes this decision from a higher perspective. You are then unable to return to your body, but you turn to face the light and are guided back into the After Life. It is a process you have probably done many times and not one to be afraid of.

Resources to Assist Your Journey

Reading List

Are you just setting out on this rewarding journey or have you been on it some time? You can find a reading list in Alison's library on her website www.yoursoulfamily.com with choices appropriate for where you are in your spiritual development. The list is not exhaustive but will give you a good range to get started with – resources that both I and Andrea found helpful.

Free Soul Map Templates and Guidance on How to Create Your First Soul Map

You can find Soul Map templates and guidance on creating your Soul Map on www.yoursoulfamily.com/soul-map-7-steps-to-understanding-you-and-your-life/.

Why would you want a Soul Map? A soul family is a group of people which can include individuals from your biological family, an adopted family, your in-laws, friends, work colleagues and even neighbours. All of these people can provide you with challenges and therefore with opportunities to learn. They might also share moments of kindness, enabling you to practice receiving. Both situations are opportunities for personal development and growth. Creating your own Soul Map helps you to consciously understand all these relationships in your life and what you

you need to learn from them. This understanding can improve your rate of learning.

Reflection for Calmness

In the 21st-century people lead busy lives, and often you feel that you have little space in which you can contemplate and just 'be'. Meditation helps to calm the noisy chatter of the mind and create the space to just 'be' and connect with your soul. You can find one of Alison's meditations aimed at assisting you to feel free and relaxed at https://soundcloud.com/user-834948611/guided-meditation-saling-alison-wem).

Guided Meditations

Meditations are a good way to experience your inner calmness when you are setting out. Listening to guided meditations develops the practice of going within and exploring your inner landscape. Many good meditations can be found on the internet. Here is the link to Alison's meditations: https://soundcloud.com/search?q=Alisonwem. Eventually you will be able to sit in silence, go within and find your space of calmness and peace. Here it is easier to commune with your soul and remember your own personal wisdom gained from living your life. These guided meditations are also good if you are an experienced meditator but fancy a change from just sitting in silence.

Life and Living Blog

Both written and video blogs are available. They promote thought from a higher perspective and offer guidance on a whole range of everyday topics, including life challenges, nature, emotions and lifting your consciousness. Give it a try and join in the debate. Meet other like-minded people to join you on your journey, at yoursoulfamily.com (https://www.yoursoulfamily.com). Sign up for Alison's newsletter for the story of the month and the most-read articles.

After Words from Lucinda

Spirit guide to Alison

Andrea and Alison have worked diligently to discover and explore their inner landscapes. In that calm centred space within, they have come to appreciate the value of the life experiences they have had and the opportunities they have given them to gain wisdom. They have truthfully tried to share it with you, so you might come to know it as well.

It really doesn't matter if you remember your life experiences in one or many lives – whatever it is, know it has contributed to who you are today. Try to own it and treasure it. Take the time now to look back on your life and see how far you have come. Treasure each little step you have taken to improve yourself as a human being and look forward to the steps that are to come.

Earth can be a hard, cruel place to live. As the upliftment of humanity's consciousness occurs and you become more aware of the expanded consciousness across Mother Earth, the Universe and beyond, life values will shift. Whether you are a man or a woman, rich or poor, a person of colour or not, or of a particular faith will become less relevant. The life values you choose to adopt and live by will be more significant than your heritage. You and who you are as a person will become key. Many perceived injustices will shift. The attachment to material success and wealth will become less prized. This change will happen over an extended period, but for you as an individual reading this book, there is no better time for making change than now.

Epilogue from Andrea

Many people have asked me how I have come to remember so many of my past lives. The easy answer is curiosity. I have investigated many ways of connecting with Universal Energy. Each time I have asked simple questions about ways of living and how I could live my life more comfortably and with greater joy. When I have asked a simple, straightforward question the answer has arrived over time. Often the memory of a past life is used to help to give the answer and to show me I already knew the answer deep within. Through this approach I have slowly understood the learnings from my lives and have started to tap into the wisdom from all of this living. This wisdom was hard-earned, so it makes sense to make use of it.

Should you want to experiment with remembering past lives and the wisdom gained from them, here are some steps Alison and I have used that you might like to try.

1. **Trigger.** Something in your current life makes you wonder if you have experienced it before, or perhaps you are wondering if you have previously learnt a skill or lesson which could help you today with a challenge.

   Or if, as Alison was, you are exploring something such as the use of sound to enhance your connection with Universal Energy, ask a question relating to it – for example, 'When has sound helped me to connect?'

2. **Focused attention.** Connect with your soul, perhaps through walking alone in nature or meditating. Ensure that you find that centred calm spot in your inner landscape where you can hear or feel the answer to your question.

   Alison and I attended a lecture by Jill Purce on chanting. Jill led the audience in a chant and we felt very connected to each other and our inner selves.

3. **A simple, clear question.** Alison asked, 'Chanting is interesting and I definitely feel more connected, but when has chanting been important to me in a life experience?'

4. **Answer retrieval.** Alison's soul quickly reviews her lives and gives her a memory of being a North American black slave working in a gang lifting and shifting heavy items. She is given a scene and the gang is chanting. There is no more detailed information.

5. **Wait for detail.** Alison thanks her soul and lets the question be. She waits one to two weeks and thinks of the slave gang a couple of times but nothing more comes.

6. **Detail arrives.** Alison now has a knowing of that life and scene and is able to write the following paragraph, plus see the scene and feel how she felt at that time. She senses and knows the scene but does not experience the actual pain of that life. If it does start to arrive, she promptly states that this is a memory and not pain to be experienced in this life. It promptly withdraws.

Here is Alison's account of that life remembered.

Black Virginian Slave Life: Man Feeling Weak and Alone

I am a black Virginian, a North American slave working in a gang assisting in the construction of large buildings and possibly ships. The gang has to lift heavy wooden logs and planks, carry them to the right place in the building and then place them into position. There is no skill in this work. We are just providing the muscle power to lift and shift. We are cheap labour doing much of what machinery would be used to do today. The work is long, hard and boring. My life is one of hard labour and endurance. When I stand in line with my gang, the man in front of me has a strong and beautiful body, much like a weightlifter today. His smooth black skin shines with the glisten of sweat from his labour. His arms are thick and muscular, his back broad and strong. By comparison I feel puny and wish for some help. My arms ache and my back hurts. I find it challenging work physically. The foreman of our gang uses chanting to synchronise our efforts – lift, shift, shift, shift, place. We turn the instructions into a song and chant. The chanting brings benefits I am not expecting. Engaging with the song and hearing my own voice lifts the boredom of the task, moves my thoughts away from the pain in my body and eases the pain, the labour becomes bearable as I tap into some unknown energy. I no longer feel so puny.

Lessons

Alison was given this chain gang life as an example of sound aiding her connection to Universal Energy.

Later when she was experimenting with crystal grids to learn how they influenced energy, she used a smooth black stone in one of her grids to symbolise being grounded and feeling strong. When Alison felt agitated over something in her life, she used to take this stone into her left hand, rest it on her fingers and feel its smoothness and strength with her thumb to help her feel her own inner strength. After a while she noticed a figure was appearing on the stone. It was the slaveowner from this Virginian life making himself known to her. He had come to explain that he had come to regret owning slaves, as over time he realised it was wrong to use people against their wishes and without reward. It was almost as if he were apologising for his lack of awareness in Virginian times.

The lessons Alison took from this are:

- *Chanting does magnify the link with your companions and your soul.*
- *When help is asked for, it can arrive in unexpected ways.*
- *Your own strength is available to you if you seek it.*

Until recently I have always been looking backwards at past lives. It is said that how you live your life today will affect the future lives you will have the opportunity to live. It is also said that in the wider reality of life, your soul is focusing on seven lives – the three most recent past lives, your current life and three potential future lives. Your soul is reviewing the past lives to see what still needs to be learnt, how the life lessons are going in your current life, and planning what life lessons need to go into future lives to maintain your momentum of learning. So, I asked this question:

> *'From where I am in my life today, what future lives might I get the chance to lead?'*

The answer arrived in the form of two examples:

Energy Teacher

In my current life I have spent much time remembering how to connect with Universal Energy to be of service to others. Initially it was about improving my education but eventually I remembered how to connect and hold the energy so others might also have the opportunity to experience it for healing, increased well-being and gaining a greater understanding of the wider reality of life.

Therefore, it came as no surprise that in a future life I might be an energy teacher. It is at a time when humanity has uplifted its consciousness and no longer eats animals but instead sustain themselves, initially from plants, but then by directly connecting to Universal Energy. I am an energy teacher and show young people how to consciously connect and create a drink which they can ingest. Everybody is capable of doing this, as the connection is initiated at the point a baby is conceived and a new life comes into this world. This is the scene I was given:

It came as no surprise that in a future life I might be an energy teacher.

I am a man who looks rather like Professor Snape in the *Harry Potter* films. I am single, rather serious and have dark straggly hair. However, I know a lot about energy and how to connect and hold it in your hands. I am wearing an emerald green suit which is both light and comfortable to wear and seems to keep me at just the right temperature. When I look around at the countryside there are no farm animals and many more trees. Where there is grass it is a lovely vibrant green. Earth is looking good and feeling vibrant. There are a number of small villages around, but they do not contain many people. The human population seems much smaller than it is today. We live in crystal houses of various colours. You can open the door to them by telepathically connecting with it and then walking through.

I have a class of three children about nine years old. Today we are learning how to connect with Universal Energy and making a substance in a tube to drink. They look like smoothies and are all the colours of the rainbow. Each child has several tubes which they are tasked to fill. It takes some concentration and control to fill each tube. Of course, the children are new to it and if the juice arrives in the tube too quickly it hits the bottom and bounces out. It sprays everywhere, over the children, onto the table and the walls around us. The children think it's great fun and are laughing heartily. I'm not so relaxed and am getting anxious about the mess we are creating. In the end I see the humour of the scene and I laugh too. I adjust what each child is doing to improve their control, and we finally have some full tubes which we can then enjoy. I liken it to learning to cook a cake and having the fun of licking the bowl.

I know I am too serious and this reduces my effectiveness at teaching. I task myself with using humour in class, as it is such a lovely light energy and enables the students to learn more easily. I have a lot of knowledge, but I am challenged in how to convey it in a way that is both interesting and fun. It is an objective of this energy teacher life to overcome this limitation.

Being single means that I have yet to overcome my other challenge. I love learning and teaching so much that I forget to live a full life myself. In many of my past lives I am a nun or a monk, as I enjoy the ecclesial life of prayer and learning. My soul is keen to help me learn these two things, as he desires lives with roles that influence and help more people. As soon as I felt this thought, another potential life scene arrived.

I am called in as a peacemaker when there is a dispute.

Peacemaker

I have a Merlin-shaped head and face but an indeterminate body. I am not sure why that is so. I am able to use thought to take myself to where I want to go. I am called in as a peacemaker when there is a dispute. When there is an argument between people in a village or between villages, the vibrational energy is out of balance and not in harmony.

On arrival at a scene of dispute, I need to use humour to lighten the energy between the individuals involved. This life must be a later life, as in the Energy Teacher life I was still grappling with humour. We then sing together as a group. Singing is like a defibrillator; it gets even beats of the heart going, from which you can build health. Singing helps to build greater harmony between people. Sadly, with church attendance and school assemblies being in decline, fewer people are getting the opportunity for regular group singing in the 21st century.

Discussion strengthens the harmony initiated through singing. Each party is allowed to speak and say how they feel without being interrupted. Giving and receiving between each of the parties helps to build consensus and agreement.

Then we dance together to cement the harmony and agreement achieved. As we repeatedly practice taking steps together to stay in tune with the music, the energy around us gains greater harmony and so the agreement is more likely to be adhered to. The John Templeton Institute, for example, supported a Science of Happiness study into the impact from moving in sync with someone else, even a total stranger, and whether it can change how you feel about them, and how you act, without your realising it.

There is the impact of moving in sync with someone else, even a total stranger, and it can change how you feel about them and how you act.

Historically many cultures have traditions of activities involving moving in synchronisation together. It is a time when you get out of your mind and more into your body and the flow of life. Modern-day equivalents include line dancing, football, body music and tai chi. When the study undertook controlled scenarios of people tapping in synch and out of synch, it was found that those tapping in synch felt more like one another and therefore more compassionate to each other. If a member of their group was in difficulty, 50 per cent of the group would be more likely to support and help them, as opposed to 20 per cent in the asynchronous group. It was found that compassion is tied to feelings of similarity.

Moving in synchronicity together weakened the boundaries between one another and increased compassion. This capability made the group stronger and was clearly crucial to successful human evolution.

I find it interesting that many of the activities humanity has undertaken for thousands of years are not so dissimilar to this future life I was given. Perhaps in modernising our lifestyles we have inadvertently thrown out practices which augment the quality of human life. Dancing is such fun. Personally, I find it energises me and makes me laugh, and I love doing it with another individual or in a group. Some people are quite shy about dancing for fear of making a mistake or feeling foolish. My own son is one of these! What people have forgotten is that dancing is not about perfection but about relaxation, going with the flow and enjoying doing a fun activity with other people.

In modernising our lifestyles we have inadvertently thrown out practices which augment the quality of human life.

Remembering your past lives is, I've found, much like dancing. It is about enhancing the quality of your current life. I don't know a person who does not have a challenge of some sort in their life. Remembering a skill from a past life which can help you today or a similar challenge you have previously negotiated can only help and inform you today.

I will leave you now, but before I go, I would like to say one last thing:

> *Learning to listen to my soul is the best thing I have ever done. It has made me feel more complete, has given my life guidance and purpose and brought me a lot of happiness.*

Epilogue from Alison

Brian Weiss, a bestselling author of books on past-life recall, raised my curiosity on the personal development benefits of remembering a past life and what it had to offer my current life. I thought it was wonderful to get the opportunity to remember some skills I had already learnt but forgotten about when I came into this life. What is there not to like about that? Even remembering past-life challenges and how I worked my way through them seemed like practicing life before you have to live it. Even if I had been a total failure in the past, at least it informed me on what I could do better this time around.

With these thoughts in mind, I approached one of Brian Weiss's consultants to do a past-life recall with me. Carefully installed on her couch, she led me in hypnosis to allow my veil to lift so I could remember an aspect of a previous life. She asked me to visualise a corridor with many doors in it. Each door would open onto one of my previous lives. I would be guided to open the door which would help me the most for where I was in my current life at that time. I stood in the corridor and looked at all the doors. I asked my spirit guide which one I should open. He roared with laughter and asked if I believed it would be as easy as that. His answer to my question was 'None!' No matter what the consultant said or I tried to do, not one door would open for me. I had spent my money and achieved nothing. Or had I?

I had set the intent of my desire to develop, to remember my past lives to understand more about myself. My soul realised I had set myself a quest and was open to listening to him and being guided by him. Together we would rediscover who I am, my capabilities and the reality of the Universe that we all live in. In so doing, my soul and I became much more aligned and at one together. It was my curiosity about past lives that drove my connection with Andrea, as she was already on her journey of past-life discovery.

It is said that your soul is working with between three and seven of your lives at any one time. Your soul will be looking at your most recent past life or lives to remember what you still need to learn; at your current life to appreciate the progress you are making; and at your next life / lives to plan in opportunities for learning still needing to happen and adjusting that plan as your current life unfolds. This is how the work in your current life influences your next life. Just being aware of the clues your body and emotions give you to past lives' experiences can help to increase your awareness. This can, for example, include phobias, such as Andrea's inability to wear a polo neck jumper and her claustrophobia, or pains and aches in your body.

Be like Andrea and relentlessly explore different techniques for communicating across the realms of the After Life and Earth.

If you feel you are in a similar place as me or even just considering the possibility of the existence of living many lives, my one piece of advice to you is to ensure that you remain open to exploring many avenues to find yourself. Follow your intuition, that feeling inside of you. Some people call it their gut instinct. I feel your intuition is like a radio receiver and sender, a beacon which can transmit across realms. Your soul, spirit guide or passed loved ones might use it to communicate with you. Or you may just connect to Universal Energy for the pervasive knowledge and wisdom that is all around us and available to use if we so desire.

Be like Andrea and relentlessly explore different techniques for communicating across the realms of the After Life and Earth. The more each of us do this, the more it creates a stronger bridge between us. Enjoy walking to the centre of the bridge and meeting loved ones, as in the ancient Japanese paintings of lovers meeting halfway across a bridge in a beautiful garden.

Here are some of the techniques Andrea and I have tried:

Scrying with Stones

Andrea's great-great grandfather came to her on the bridge. He was a master stonemason and had worked in cathedrals and churches. He was attracted to her as she was using a medium he loved. I learnt to throw a shaman's spread of stones to give messages hidden in the stones themselves and in their arrangement.

Crystals

Learning and feeling the energy crystals provide can enhance many aspects of your life. There is much good information on crystals freely available on the internet. Valerie Pitts in London runs some great workshops and courses. Books by the late Judy Hall provide useful reference material in an easy-to-read form with wonderful photos.

There is much to be learnt about crystals but if you have a shocking memory like me, trust your guide to pick the right crystal for you for where you are in your life. I have a bag of crystals and periodically I have a rummage in it and draw one that feels good to me. I then look up the meaning of the crystal from the catalogue I keep of each crystal I have put in my bag. I take a picture of the crystal and record the healing properties before I put it in my bag. It's a wonderful, simple way to allow crystals into your life.

Oracle Cards

These oracle cards are decks of cards with pictures and messages. It never ceases to amaze me that we always draw the right card for where we are in our life. It is the same if I request to draw one on behalf of a client as I work with them online. Every time I do it, it gives me childish delight, like opening a surprise present.

Guided Meditation

Andrea and I have become regular practitioners of meditation. It feels like I'm giving myself a treat, and I always feel better afterwards. It is time well spent, and I wished I had been more aware of it when I was a busy working mum.

To explain a little more, meditation is a technique to encourage a heightened state of awareness and focused attention. It enables you to relax, reduce stress and visit your inner landscape. In a guided meditation a trusted person guides you in focusing your attention, relaxing your body and your mind. There are many well-known people and good books and podcasts which do this, including one I particularly enjoy: *True Meditation: Discover the Freedom of Pure Awareness* by Adyashanti. I have personally experienced Geoffrey Beitz in the UK, who offers great live guided meditations online. He takes you deep within yourself. You can find these meditations on the website for The College of Psychic Studies (https://www.collegeofpsychicstudies.co.uk).

Chakras

These are the spinning wheels of energy which support our mind and organs. It is good to have some understanding of our energy body, the elements within it and the benefits of it functioning at an optimum level. How you chose to live your life affects not just your physical body but your energy one as well.

Tai Chi

Energy can move around the body to increase its flexibility and strength. Tai chi is a series of gentle exercises and stretches. Each posture flows into the next without pause, ensuring that your body is in constant motion. It is sometimes described as meditation in motion, as it helps to centre you and bring in calmness and inner peace.

Healing Meditation

Healing meditations can be very powerful experiences, as I found out when I volunteered to be someone for trainee healers at the College of Psychic Studies to gain practical experience of giving healing. I had an amazing experience. It came at a low point in my life when my husband was undergoing cancer treatment. However, I felt very uplifted by the healing and motivated to get on with my life no matter what was happening in it.

Soul Maps

A Soul Map is a visual representation of you and your life. Your own Soul Map is like a personal mandala which shows the important people in your life, your relationship with them and the life lessons you may be learning in this lifetime. I called these diagrams Soul Maps, as they felt like a map with a route back to connecting with your own soul. When I teach creating Soul Maps, I have noticed that each is private to the individual who created it. However, if they talk me through the messages in the Soul Map, it seems to turn the key in the door and unlocks access to their soul. The Soul Map then becomes a portal to their inner landscape and I can readily talk with their soul.

It is a wonderful tool that helps me to assist people to commence conscious communication with their soul. It is rather like learning to read your first book in primary school and has the same wonder of opening up a whole set of experiences you would not otherwise have the opportunity to enjoy. Try the short, simple book *Creating Your Soul Map* to create your first Soul Map to start to unlock your soul. *Finding Your Soul Family* goes into much more depth in exploring the life lessons you are learning and who is helping you with learning them.

Ancient Cultures

Many of these cultures hold the truth on our eternal lives and connection with one another. Examples include:

Gregg Braden, who has done much research into ancient cultures and their practices and relates them to modern scientific discoveries.

Karen Newell of Sacred Acoustics experimented with sounds such as gongs, crystal bowls and tuning forks. It was found that recordings with binaural beats[22] were particularly effective at minimising distracting thoughts and

22 **Binaural beats:** A perception of sound created by your brain. If you listen to two tones, each at a different frequency and each in a different ear, your brain creates an additional tone you can hear. This third tone is called a binaural beat. You hear it at the frequency difference between the two tones.

restlessness, allowing you to finally reach the expanded states of awareness some seek.

Jill Purce of Healing Voice has brought ancient Mongolian overtone chanting to the attention of many. Overtone chanting is a set of singing techniques in which the vocalist manipulates the resonances of the vocal tract in order to arouse the perception of additional, separate notes beyond the fundamental frequency being produced. To me it sounds like angelic bells rising above the chant.

Many of our spiritual leaders gain their fundamental understanding of the reality of life from ancient cultures. Modern sciences of measurement and our attempts to include all, such as banning assembles at the start of the school day as it was perceived to be Christian in a multidenominational country, seem to have driven out good practices like singing together to help achieve harmony. I feel we have rather thrown the baby out with the bathwater and we need to re-address this need. Reflection back on ancient cultures can help to bring us back into harmony with Earth and each other.

Reiki

Reiki is a healing technique based on the principle that the therapist can channel energy into the patient by means of touch, in order to activate the natural healing processes of the patient's body and restore physical and emotional well-being. Taken more broadly, reiki is energy healing. The practitioner needs to learn to connect with Universal Energy, which is intelligent love that knows what the patient needs. The healer holds the energy for the patient to accept or reject whatever they need. Learning to connect and hold intelligent energy in your hands is a journey in itself. It is rewarding, and loving, yet at the same time it is challenging. It asks of you to be your best and purest self, which is a quest in its own right.

Esoteric Natal Astrology Chart

Esoteric astrology or, as it is sometimes called, soul-centred astrology, and the symbols within it give the rational mind an understanding of both external events and the qualities of the soul. Therefore, esoteric astrology is a successful interpreter of human evolution and events. An esoteric natal chart is of the soul rather than the personality. It reflects what qualities the soul brings to this life and also what it is seeking to achieve. The placement of Saturn in your chart is an indication of the area in your life which you wish to work on.

Andrea: Many of the core capabilities I felt I could bring to my life situations were indeed from my soul. I did not realise this until I had an esoteric natal chart created for me. Amongst my surprises were the desire for right relationships, being decisive and increased awareness of the soul. The intentions of my soul for this life included being grounded and practical, an inclination to hard work and detail, the desire to face into the shadow areas of myself and address them. There were no major surprises into my nature, but I found it was interesting and perhaps a little surprising on how much of my life was influenced by my soul.

Alison: These are but a few possible lines of investigation on the journey to find yourself. Choose whichever ones you feel attracted to. They are in the order we tried them, but that doesn't make them the right order for you. Just ask a question quietly of yourself if you would like to investigate any of these topics. I hope some of these suggestions will help you to think about what would be good for you and your spiritual development.

Note from the Author

If you have loved the book and have a moment to spare, it would mean the world to me if you took two minutes to share your thoughts about this book. You can leave a review of *Secrets of Your Soul* on Amazon at https://www.amazon.com/author/alisonwem and/or send me an email with your honest feedback to alison.wem@yoursoulfamily.com.

Your feedback helps me provide the best-quality books and helps other readers like you discover great books.

Your help in spreading the word is gratefully received.

Love and Light,
Alison

YOUR SOUL FAMILY

connecting with your soul
calmness – harmony - wisdom

Acknowledgements

I would like to thank my parents, *Ronald and Elizabeth Holloway*, for the gift they gave me of a happy childhood. Their strong life values, harmony and love gave me a strong foundation on which I could live my life.

Thank you also to my husbands, *Howard Pooley* and *Douglas Wem*. Both are generous men who have supported my endeavours in different ways. Howard's unconditional love gave me strength. Douglas has accepted my living an inner life alongside us living an outer physical one.

Thank you to my children, *Nicholas Pooley* and *Rebecca Scher*, who have supported me throughout my endeavours, especially when I decided to go public on my beliefs.

Thank you to my stepchildren *Jennifer, Alasdair* and *Eleanor Wem* who helped me to appreciate that love is expansive and you don't need to be related by blood to love someone.

Thank you to *Alistair Wem*, my lovely father-in-law, who accepted me as family when I most needed it and reinforced the value of family, whether by blood or in-laws or soul family.

Lastly and not least is *Andrea*. Our friendship started with our mutual experience of widowhood. Little did we know then how deep this friendship would go. Thank you, Andrea, for finding the courage to be so honest about your life experiences so we might all learn from you.

About Alison Wem

After a successful corporate career balanced with raising a family, Alison Wem left her job to pursue her true dream of helping people lead happier, healthier and more prosperous lives. Alison uses her energy to offer healing, provide life guidance through psychic mediumship readings, teaches psychic mediumship and provides creative workshops to help people to know their soul family and to experience connecting with their soul.

Alison moved forward from widowhood to find an inner strength and wisdom she did not know she possessed. She did this through going within, the subject of her book *Creating Your Soul Map*.

Books by Alison

Creating Your Soul Map

Do you need a Soul Map? For Alison Wem, that realisation came in the early hours one night as, newly widowed and with children and a demanding job, she confronted her anguish – and found not chaos and more pain but a space of calmness and route to strength, love and guidance.

In this first book Alison provides easy-to-do steps in creating your own Soul Map – a route back to your inner landscape and your 'inner you' – your subconscious mind, higher self, or soul, depending on your beliefs.

> *'Alison provides a unique insight into gaining more understanding of yourself and improving your overall happiness at home and work. I look forward to reading more books in the series!'*
>
> – *Sean Lampert,* Amazon Reader

The Your Soul Family website, https://www.yoursoulfamily.com, has examples of Soul Maps and how to quickly create one for yourself, and includes free Soul Map templates.

Finding Your Soul Family

Are you looking to feel more connected to those you love? Do you want to feel more alive, vibrant and healthy? Or are you simply looking to find deeper meaning and richness in your life?

Alison Wem offers a new approach to managing stress and anxiety in our 21st-century lives. *Finding Your Soul Family* provides you with techniques to help you know yourself better and to enhance your sense of personal calmness so you can be more effective at work and live more harmoniously at home.

> *'If you enjoyed Alison Wem's previous title,* Creating Your Soul Map, *you will love this follow-up. This book is specifically about finding your soul family. It is beautifully put together with images and illustrations that clarify the techniques and ideas described. There are many resources and exercises here and you can return to the book again and again, especially when you're going through tough choices or feeling disconnected from spiritual guidance. A practical and well-thought-out way to reconnect with yourself and with the Divine.''*
>
> – Kindred Spirit Magazine *review*

Life and Living Blog

Alison Wem talks and writes about everyday life and its challenges. Easy to read and inspiring, her posts help you get through your day in a way that honours yourself.

You can get updates on the best articles each month by subscribing at https://yoursoulfamily.com.

YOUR SOUL FAMILY

connecting with your soul

calmness – harmony - wisdom

From Alison Wem's *Creating Your Soul Map*

Preface

I came to Your Soul Family some years ago. In the space of three years all of my near family passed away except for my brother, who was a six-hour journey away. The hardest passing was when I was unexpectedly widowed. My son was then fifteen years old and my daughter had just had her eleventh birthday party. I really did not know how I was going to cope with raising two children alone, running a home and holding down a demanding full-time job. I was on the go from 6 a.m. to 11 p.m. and then not sleeping well. I knew that this pace was not sustainable, but I did not know how to change my life. I felt so alone and unloved.

Many readers will have had similar experiences of bereavement, or extreme stress that can arise from any number of situations. Many of them involve loss of someone or something you value – a child, partner, job, business, home. Each of us needs to find a way of handling our loss or stress.

It was in the early hours of a morning when sleep eluded me that I stumbled on my inner consciousness and found a space of calmness. It was there that I let out all of my hurt and loneliness – but to my great surprise it was there that I found strength, love and guidance. At last I had met my 'inner you'. Some people call this 'inner you' your sub-conscious, higher self or soul, depending on their life view. I like 'inner you' as it feels more familiar, someone close to you and not ethereal.

Meeting my 'inner you' was a real turning point for me. My key question was

What should I do next in my life?

I knew I could not continue my life as it was, but I did not know how to change it for the better. Over time, my 'inner you' guided me in making small changes that made my life more manageable.

One of the life lessons I needed to learn was to be able to receive. I had always been a capable person, usually the one organising others and giving of myself. It took the dramatic event of becoming a widow to make me realise that I needed to be more balanced and to receive as well as to give. It was a hard life lesson for me, and it did not come to me easily. In the early months of widowhood, I survived through the kindness of friends, through their practical gifts of collecting a child from school, fixing things in the home when they went wrong, providing a meal when I was exhausted and calling me so I did not feel so alone.

After I first stumbled on my place of calmness, it took me some time to learn to communicate with my 'inner you'. It required trial and error plus repeating things many times over a number of weeks to see if I received the same answers. It took me some time to get to know my 'inner you' and to learn to trust the messages I received.

To make your journey easier, the Your Soul Family series of books captures the processes of getting to know your 'inner you', so you too can have a friend to aid you as you encounter challenges on your journey of life. In this process you will create and colour a geometric picture of you and your life which I have called a 'Soul Map', as a visual aid to understanding yourself better. No artistic skills are required.

Through a number of exercises, you will get to know your 'inner you' and learn to ask simple questions to receive your own wisdom. This guide with its simple-to-follow steps is the first in this series. I strongly believe that your 'inner you' will enrich your life and will guide you in enhancing your own personal development.

No matter where you are in life's journey, no-one is too old, too clever or too wise to learn new things. Your Soul Family is a new approach to personal development which bridges the scientific approaches of the 20th century and the mystical approaches of past ages to help us to cope with the bustle of living in the 21st century.

Give it a try with this short book, which provides easy-to-follow steps in creating your Soul Map to meet your 'inner you'.

Best wishes,
Alison Wem

Printed in Great Britain
by Amazon

46440072R00123